Hervé Champollion

Wonderful
FRANCE

Photographs by the author
Translated by Angela Moyon

ÉDITIONS OUEST-FRANCE
13, rue du Breil, Rennes

BY THE SAME AUTHOR

The Brière Marshes (Ouest-France, 1981).
Vivre Paris (Mengès, 1987).
L'Egypte de J-F. Champollion (CELIV, 1993).
La photographie (Ouest-France, 1991).
Frankreich. In collaboration with Wilhelm Ziehr (Reich Verlag, Lucerne, 1984).
*Sizilien.*In collaboration with Wilhelm Ziehr (Pinguin, Innsbruck, 1988).
Jérusalem. In collaboration with Louis Estrangin *(Ouest-France, 1987).*

BIBLIOGRAPHY

Géographie régionale de la France, Georges Chabot (Masson, Paris).
Art d'Occident, Henri Focillon (Armand Colin, Paris).
Ouest-France colour guides collection (Edilarge Editions, Rennes).
Green Guide to France (Michelin, Paris).

Top : **Caylus** (Quercy).

Middle : **Douarnenez** (Brittany).

Bottom : **Albion Plateau** (Upper Provence).

Front cover :
The R. Dordogne in Castelnaud.

Back cover :
Mont-Saint-Michel.

With its well-balanced layout, temperate climate, geographical area that,
although extensive, remains human, coastline facing four different seas, and its situation
as a lynch-pin between Northern Europe and the Mediterranean Basin, France has a unique
variety of landscapes to offer its people and its visitors. From the high peaks of the Alps and
Pyrenees to the plains in Flanders, from the pastures of Normandy to the volcanoes
of Auvergne, from the rugged coastline of Brittany to the vineyards of Alsace, Burgundy
and the Bordeaux area, the abundance and diversity of the scenery, some of it natural,
some of it shaped by the hand of Man, offers the subtle pleasures
of constant change to those who really know how to look.
The epic period of Romanesque monasteries, the daring experiments dating
from the Gothic era and the great century of Classicism have produced countless examples
of the genius of their designers and builders. This is the visible heritage of French civilisation,
and it is this heritage which this book intends to show and explain, by setting
it in its historical and geographical context.

Old French provinces. Languages and dialects. Landscapes and agriculture.

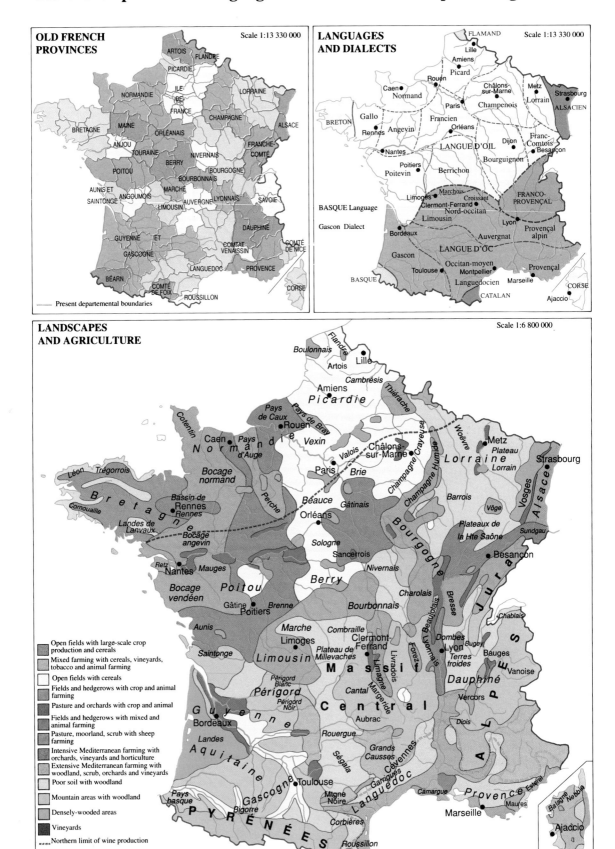

OLD FRENCH PROVINCES
Scale 1:13 330 000

ARTOIS
FLANDRE
PICARDIE
NORMANDIE
ILE-DE-FRANCE
LORRAINE
CHAMPAGNE
ALSACE
BRETAGNE
MAINE
ORLÉANAIS
ANJOU
TOURAINE
FRANCHE-COMTÉ
BERRY
NIVERNAIS
POITOU
BOURGOGNE
BOURBONNAIS
AUNIS ET SAINTONGE
ANGOUMOIS
MARCHE
AUVERGNE
LYONNAIS
SAVOIE
LIMOUSIN
DAUPHINÉ
GUYENNE ET GASCOGNE
COMTAT VENAISSIN
COMTÉ DE NICE
BÉARN
LANGUEDOC
PROVENCE
COMTÉ DE FOIX
ROUSSILLON
CORSE

— Present departemental boundaries

LANGUAGES AND DIALECTS
Scale 1:13 330 000

FLAMAND
Lille
Amiens
Picard
Rouen
Caen
Normand
Châlons-sur-Marne
Metz
Lorrain
Strasbourg
ALSACIEN
Paris
Champenois
BRETON
Gallo
Francien
Rennes
Angevin
Orléans
Dijon
Franc-Comtois
Besançon
Nantes
LANGUE D'OIL
Bourguignon
Poitiers
Poitevin
Berrichon
BASQUE Language
Limoges
Marchois
Croissant
Clermont-Ferrand
Nord-occitan
FRANCO-PROVENÇAL
Gascon Dialect
Limousin
Lyon
Bordeaux
Auvergnat
Provençal alpin
Gascon
LANGUE D'OC
Occitan-moyen
Montpellier
Provençal
Toulouse
Languedocien
Marseille
BASQUE
CATALAN
CORSE
Ajaccio

LANDSCAPES AND AGRICULTURE
Scale 1:6 800 000

Flandre
Boulonnais
Lille
Artois
Cambrésis
Amiens
Picardie
Thiérache
Pays de Caux
Rouen
Pays de Bray
Cotentin
Caen
Pays d'Auge
Vexin
Valois
Châlons-sur-Marne
Champagne Crayeuse
Woëvre
Metz
Plateau Lorrain
Strasbourg
Normandie
Paris
Brie
Lorraine
Bocage normand
Perche
Béauce
Gâtinais
Champagne Humide
Barrois
Vôge
Vosges
Alsace
Léon
Trégorrois
Bassin de Rennes
Rennes
Orléans
Plateaux de la Hte Saône
Sundgau
Bretagne
Cornouaille
Landes de Lanvaux
Bocage angevin
Sologne
Sancerrois
Bourgogne
Besançon
Jura
Retz
Nantes
Mauges
Berry
Nivernais
Charolais
Bresse
Chablais
Bocage vendéen
Poitou
Gâtine
Brenne
Bourbonnais
Beaujolais
Dombes
Bugey
Bauges
Poitiers
Aunis
Marche
Combraille
Clermont-Ferrand
Limagne
Lyonnais
Lyon
Terres froides
Vanoise
Limoges
Plateau de Millevaches
Massif
Livradois
Forez
Dauphiné
Saintonge
Limousin
Cantal
Margeride
Vercors
Périgord Blanc
Central
Diois
Périgord Noir
Périgord
Aubrac
Guyenne
Bordeaux
Rouergue
Alpes
Landes
Ségala
Grands Causses
Aquitaine
Gascogne
Mtgne Noire
Cévennes
Garrigues
Languedoc
Camargue
Provence
Esterel
Balagne
Nebbio
Pays basque
Toulouse
Maures
Marseille
Bigorre
PYRÉNÉES
Corbières
Ajaccio
Roussillon

Legend:
- Open fields with large-scale crop production and cereals
- Mixed farming with cereals, vineyards, tobacco and animal farming
- Open fields with cereals
- Fields and hedgerows with crop and animal farming
- Pasture and orchards with crop and animal
- Fields and hedgerows with mixed and animal farming
- Pasture, moorland, scrub with sheep farming
- Intensive Mediterranean farming with orchards, vineyards and horticulture
- Extensive Mediterranean farming with woodland, scrub, orchards and vineyards
- Poor soil with woodland
- Mountain areas with woodland
- Densely-wooded areas
- Vineyards
- ···· Northern limit of wine production
- ···· Northern limit of olive growing

History and Architecture

Engraving on reindeer antler, 15000 - 10000 B.C.
(Les Eyzies Museum, Dordogne).

Vienne : Temple of Augustus and Livia,
1st Century B.C.

Vézelay : The capital showing the mystic mill,
early 12th Century.

35000 - 10000 B.C. The birth of Homo Sapiens. **Dordogne and Vézère Valleys**: cave paintings (*p. 101*).

4500 - 2000 B.C. The Stone Age civilisation develops in **Brittany** (*p.62*) and **Corsica** (*p.157*).

59 - 51 B.C. Gaul, whose indigenous peoples came originally from Celtic lands and Iberia, is conquered by Julius Caesar. The Gallo-Roman civilisation leaves behind buildings of immense architectural value. In the 3rd Century, the barbarian invasions sweep through the country, leaving a trail of devastation.

481 - 511 A.D. Clovis, King of the Franks, is baptised in **Rheims** in 498 A.D.

800 A.D. The Coronation of Charlemagne, who established the vast Holy Roman Empire. The Treaty of Verdun, signed in 843 A.D, divided his empire into three sections. Francia Occidentalis, lying to the west of the rivers Scheldt, Meuse and Rhône, becomes known as France.

987 A.D. Hugh Capet mounts the throne of France.

11th Century - mid 12th Century. The weakness of central government leads to the establishment of the feudal system and the lords of the land begin building their fortresses. The strengthening of the Christian faith is evident from the increase in the numbers of churches, monasteries and priories being built. The forms are simple and the volumes harmonious. Creativity is obvious in the inven-

Saint-Benoît-sur-Loire :
The Romanesque doorway, 12th Century.

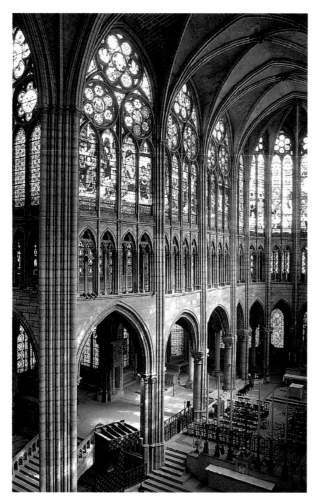

Saint-Denis : The chancel in the cathedral,
12th - 13th Century.

Vaux-le-Vicomte : Mid 17th Century.

tive, skilful carvings that are a major feature of Romanesque architecture.

Mid 12th Century - 13th Century. Mediaeval civilisation reaches its height, with a population explosion, the development of towns, the improvement of farmland, and a new thirst for knowledge. This is a period of progress, marked by the building of audaciously-designed cathedrals, particularly in the Paris Basin. By using quadripartite vaulting to bear the thrust, the walls are no longer vital load-bearing elements and light can be allowed to flood into the buildings through huge stained glass windows.

1337 - 1475. The One Hundred Years' War, fought against a background of abject poverty and unrest, sees the Capetian monarchs attempt to push back the English. Du Guesclin re-establishes law and order, and Joan of Arc liberates Orleans in 1429. The Treaty of Picquigny (1475) signed by Louis XI puts an end to the hostilities.

16th Century. Despite the religious crisis caused by the Reformation, France is swept by a desire for revival and renewal in every sector. The Renaissance leads to the development of Humanism and a refined lifestyle symbolised by the castles in the Loire Valley.

1643 - 1715. The reign of Louis XIV, the "Sun King", is a time of military glory (France was the leading power in Europe), literary fame (Molière, Racine, Boileau, and La Fontaine) and artistic excellence (Mansart, Le Brun). The Palace of Versailles (*p.13*) is a symbol of the triumph of absolute monarchy, which is seen as a synthesis of the driving forces that surrounded the sovereign. Classical architecture (the orderly distribution of mass) is an expression of controlled passions; it is replaced by the Baroque style that makes light of any rules (volumes overlap, symmetry is no longer *de rigueur*, architecture includes curves and sculptures). The end of the 18th Century is marked by a return to an academic style and Neo-Classical architecture combines new techniques with the magnificence of designs dating back to the days of Ancient Greece and Rome.

1789 - 1793. A long financial, social and political crisis puts an end to pre-Revolutionary France. Louis XVI goes to the guillotine on 21st January 1793.

1804 - 1815. Napoleon Bonaparte is crowned Emperor of the French People in **Paris** (*p. 28*) and completes the administrative re-structuring of France. The wars against European coalitions result in his abdication in Fontainebleau (*p. 15*) and his defeat at Waterloo, and weaken the country generally.

1815 - 1848. After the restoration of the monarchy (Louis XVIII and Charles X), Louis-Philippe establishes a constitutional monarchy but is deposed in February 1848.

1848 - 1870. The Second Republic is replaced, in 1851, by the Second Empire. The reign of Napoleon III is marked by the spread of the Industrial Revolution, made possible thanks to the increased use of machinery and the mining of coal and iron. The disastrous war against Prussia leads, in 1871, to the loss of Alsace and part of Lorraine.

1871 - 1939. The Third Republic implements a number of major reforms. Primary education becomes free and mandatory for all, trades unions are given official status, and the Roman Catholic Church is no longer the established church. Foreign policy concentrates on colonial expansion. The Great War (1914 - 1918) ends in victory aver Germany but it bleeds France white. New needs (department stores, railway stations, exhibition centres) and revolutionary new techniques (metal structures) produce architecture designed to make optimum use of existing land while providing ever-increasing areas of development.

1939 - 1945. Second World War.

1945 - . The modernisation of the country and the building of Europe are the main priorities of the Fourth and Fifth Republics. The use of new building materials (concrete (*p. 22*), aluminium and glass) widens the scope of architectural creativity.

Assy Plateau (Upper Savoie) : *The Passing of the Red Sea* by Chagall (1887 - 1985).

Paris : The Napoleon Courtyard in the Louvre and the Pyramid designed by L-M. Pei.

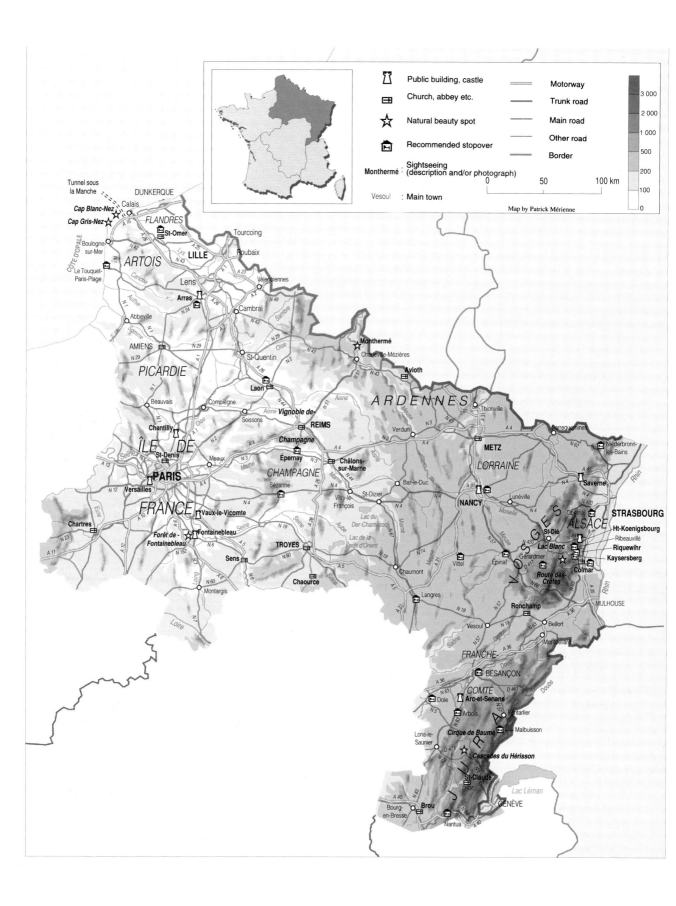

Public building, castle
Church, abbey etc.
Natural beauty spot
Recommended stopover
Monthermé : Sightseeing (description and/or photograph)
Vesoul : Main town

Motorway
Trunk road
Main road
Other road
Border

0   50   100 km

Map by Patrick Mérienne

3 000
2 000
1 000
500
200
100
0

Tunnel sous la Manche
DUNKERQUE
Cap Blanc-Nez
Cap Gris-Nez
Calais
FLANDRES
St-Omer
Tourcoing
Boulogne-sur-Mer
Côte d'Opale
LILLE
Roubaix
ARTOIS
Le Touquet-Paris-Plage
Lens
Valenciennes
Arras
Cambrai
Abbeville
St-Quentin
AMIENS
PICARDIE
Laon
Beauvais
Compiègne
Chantilly
Soissons
Aisne
Vignoble de-
ARDENNES
Monthermé
Charleville-Mézières
Avioth
Thionville
Verdun
Reims
ÎLE DE
St-Denis
Meaux
Champagne
Épernay
Châlons-sur-Marne
METZ
LORRAINE
Serrequemines
Niederbronn-les-Bains
PARIS
Versailles
CHAMPAGNE
Sézanne
Vitry-le-François
Bar-le-Duc
NANCY
Lunéville
Saverne
Obernai
STRASBOURG
FRANCE
Vaux-le-Vicomte
St-Dizier
Chartres
Fontainebleau
Forêt de-Fontainebleau
TROYES
Lac du-Der-Chantecoq
Lac de la-Forêt d'Orient
Chaumont
Vittel
St-Dié
ALSACE
Ht-Koenigsbourg
Lac Blanc
Ribeauvillé
Riquewihr
Kaysersberg
Colmar
Sens
Épinal
Gérardmer
Route des-Crêtes
VOSGES
MULHOUSE
Chaource
Montargis
Langres
Ronchamp
Vesoul
Bellfort
Montbéliard
FRANCHE-COMTÉ
BESANÇON
Arc-et-Senans
Dole
Arbois
Fontarlier
Malbuisson
Lons-le-Saunier
Cirque de Baume
Cascades du Hérisson
St-Claude
JURA
Bourg-en-Bresse
Brou
Nantua
Lac Léman
GENÈVE

NORTH-EASTERN FRANCE

Paris Basin, Franche-Comté, Alsace, Lorraine, Champagne, Flanders, Artois, Picardy.

The park in **Versailles**.

Kaysersberg in Alsace.

Ever since the Capetian monarchs chose **Paris** as their capital in the 12th Century, the city has acquired countless prestigious buildings, a reminder of its political and economic importance. The castles, parks and cathedrals in the Paris Basin also bear witness to its eventful past.

The mountains in the **Jura** form a crescent lying in a south to north-easterly direction and cover most of the old Franche-Comté region. Beyond the mountain ranges in the south and east are a succession of limestone plateaux gashed by valleys and gorges. A multitude of springs, rivers and lakes add a touch of freshness to scenery that inspired both Lamartine and Goethe.

The **Vosges** with their characteristic rounded hilltops (the Ballons) are mainly covered in forest, with alpine pastures (the *Hautes Chaumes*) above. The valleys in the Vosges provide a link with the Alsace Plain. The 20-mile wide corridor resembles one vast garden consisting of drained marshland and winding rivers, now covered with orchards and meadows. The foothills of the Vosges bear the Alsace vineyards.

The **plateaux of Lorraine** are flanked to the west by **Champagne**, an area that is world-famous for its sparkling wine. Further north, the rolling green hills of the **Ardennes** are crossed by the winding course of the R. Meuse.

The **Plateau in Picardy** broken up by valleys and dotted with lakes and the plains of **Artois** are an extension of the Paris Basin. The plain in **Flanders** is a low-lying region with scattered country cottages. The slag heaps of the "black country" are the last reminders of the vast coalfields that were mined from the 18th Century onwards.

Notre-Dame, and the **Quais de Béthune and Orléans**. The Ile de la Cité, the historic centre of Paris, and the Ile Saint-Louis, are filled with a number of outstanding buildings. Notre-Dame Cathedral, built from 1163 to 1345, is one of the finest examples of French Gothic architecture thanks to the wonderfully well-balanced proportions.

A stroll round the quaysides in the Ile Saint-Louis is one of the most delightful walks in Paris. It gives an opportunity to see the superb 17th and 18th-century mansions and the Marie Bridge. From the Quai d'Orléans, there is an interesting view of the chevet of Notre-Dame.

The Sainte-Chapelle. Built on the orders of St. Louis in the mid 13th Century to house relics of Christ and the Virgin Mary, this is a veritable piece of lacework in stone and glass. The stained glass windows in the upper chapel, illustrating 134 scenes from the Bible, are the oldest in Paris (13th Century).

The Champs-Elysées. The Champs-Elysées stretch from the Place de la Concorde, adorned with one of the obelisks from Luxor given to France by the Viceroy of Egypt, Muhammad 'Ali in 1829 during a visit by Champollion, to the Place Charles-de-Gaulle dominated by the Arc de Triomphe (1806 - 1836). This is the most prestigious avenue in the world and it extends into the Tuileries Gardens at one end and the Avenue de la Grande-Armée at the other. Over a distance of several miles, there is a succession of luxury shops, head offices of major companies, cinemas and concert halls.

The Arc de Triomphe, commissioned by Napoleon and dedicated to the imperial army, was designed to resemble the buildings of Ancient Greece and Rome. The haut-relief known as *The Marseillaise* (to the right on the East side) is a masterpiece by Rude. It represents the departure of the volunteers in 1792. Because of its irresistible sense of movement, it far outclasses the other sculptures created by Cortot and Etex.

The Eiffel Tower. Built in two years for the 1889 World Fair to designs by an engineer named Gustave Eiffel, this 975-foot metal tower aroused a wave of protest among the artists and literary figures of the day. It only just escaped demolition in 1909 but has since become the best-known of all the sights in Paris. First and foremost, though, it is a masterpiece of metalwork construction, combining lightness and strength. In storm-force winds, its top moves only 5 inches. A foot-high steel model would weigh only 7 grams.

Visitors can access all three floors. From the top, the view extends far beyond the city itself but, down below the tower, the layout of the avenues and location of the various buildings create an interesting relief map.

Right on the top of the hill is the Sacré-Coeur, built after the French defeat in the Franco-Prussian War (1870-1871) and paid for by a nationwide public subscription. It is a pastiche of Byzantine architecture and is topped with domes inspired by the ones on St. Front's Cathedral in Périgueux (*p. 99*).

Bottom : **The Place des Vosges**. Set in the heart of the Marais District, the Place des Vosges has 36 brick and stone townhouses dating from the early 17th Century; they were commissioned by King Henri IV. This was a place to enjoy oneself and lead a life of elegance but it was also a favourite place with duellists. The square led to the development of the district as a whole. Aristocrats and courtisans had luxurious mansions built here, and they formed the centre of the literary and artistic life in Paris until the French Revolution.

Top : **The Basilica of the Sacred Heart** (the *Sacré-Coeur*). During the last century, and until 1914, Montmartre was the haunt of artists and men of letters. A Bohemian lifestyle flourished on the hill, in the wake of men like Hector Berlioz and Gérard de Nerval. The "*cafés-concert*" (music halls like the *Bateau-Lavoir* or *Lapin Agile*) still ring with the songs of Aristide Bruant while the artists on the Place du Tertre take advantage of the fame of Utrillo and Picasso to offer their works to passers-by.

The regular layout of the house fronts, with their two upper storeys and arcaded ground floor, is broken to north and south by the inclusion of the King's and Queen's Mansions. The Place des Vosges was the birthplace of Mme de Sévigné (no. 1b), and Richelieu lived at no. 31. Victor Hugo's House is open to the public at no. 6; the author of *Les Misérables* lived here from 1832 to 1848.

Top : **The Palace of Versailles**. This extraordinary royal property (palace, park and Trianon) symbolise the absolute power of the monarch during the reign of Louis XIV. The extension to the small castle built for Louis XIII began in 1668 under the direction of Louis Le Vau and continued on a large scale when Jules Hardouin-Mansart launched the building of the North and South Wings in 1678. The central section of the palace contains the impressive Hall of Mirrors. Working under the orders of Charles Le Brun, the best sculptors, painters and tapestry-manufacturers of the day undertook the decoration of the royal apartments, chambers and halls, galleries, chapel and opera house. No detail was too small to escape the king's watchful eye.

The fountains are surrounded by bronze statues representing the main rivers of France (men) and their tributaries (women).

Left : **Chantilly Castle**. The present house was commissioned by the Duke d'Aumale, Louis-Philippe's fifth son, and was built between 1875 and 1885 in the Renaissance style on the ruins of an earlier castle built by the Great Condé, one of Louis XIV's most outstanding generals, and razed to the ground during the French Revolution. The works of art set out in the main castle are absolutely superb. Collected by the Duke d'Aumale, they include paintings by Raphael (*The Madonna, The Three Graces*), Botticelli (*Autumn*), and Ingres (self-portrait, *Venus Anadyomene*).

Chartres Cathedral. The Royal Entrance, towers, crypt and some of the stained glass windows in Our Lady of the Fine Window (*Notre-Dame-de-la-Belle-Verrière*) come from the Romanesque cathedral commissioned by Bishop Fulbert (11th and 12th Centuries) and destroyed by fire in 1194. The remainder of the building owes its uniformity to the rapidity with which the rebuilding was completed. It took only 25 years, with the exception of the North and South portals, which were completed c. 1260. Dedicated to the Assumption of the Virgin Mary, of whom there are no less than 175 statues or pictures, the cathedral has always attracted large crowds of pilgrims, from the vast crowds of the Middle Ages to the "Annual Students' Pilgrimage" inspired by the poet, Charles Péguy.

The **Royal Entrance** (*bottom, left*) is a masterpiece of Late Romanesque architecture, dating from the mid 12th Century. The statue-pillars showing the Prophets and the Kings and Queens of the Bible are elongated to a maximum, combining aesthetics and usefulness. The Romanesque decoration succeeded here in "replacing the proportions and harmony of life with the proportions and harmony of architectural order" (Henri Focillon, *Art d'Occident*).

The stained glass windows include more than 5,000 characters, over a surface of 2,700 sq. metres. Dating mainly from the 12th and 13th Centuries, they give the interior of the cathedral a dappled duskiness. The famous "Chartres blue" colour fills the nave with a very special atmosphere. The stained glass window of Our Lady of the Fine Window (*bottom, right*), the first bay to the right of the ambulatory, combines a whole range of blues. The luminous blue in the three central panels (12th Century) emphasises the deeper, more intense blue used by the master glass painter a century later, in the 13th.

The Palace of Fontainebleau. From the days of the Capetian monarchs who built a hunting lodge here near the forest in the 12th Century to Napoleon III, this palace was furnished and lived in by the country's monarchs without a break. François I replaced the mediaeval castle with two Renaissance buildings linked by a gallery. In the early 16th Century, attractive residences with refined decoration were fashionable. Whole teams of Italian artists (Il Rosse, Niccolo dell'Abbate, Primaticcio) created a set of stucco work and paintings that formed the background to master-pieces by Raphael and Leonardo da Vinci.

The central façade overlooking the **Horseshoe Courtyard** (*right*) is preceded by the famous horseshoe staircase with its curved flights of steps designed by Jean du Cerceau during the reign of Louis XIII. This courtyard was the setting, on 20th April 1814, for Napoleon's final farewell to his troops, after his abdication.

The **forest** (*bottom, right*) covers an area of 25,000 hectares. It includes an extensive network of footpaths leading to the finest beauty spots in the region, including the picturesque sandstone rocks that are so popular with Parisian "mountaineers".

Troyes. The Cathedral of St. Peter and St. Paul (*cathédrale de Saint-Pierre et Saint-Paul*) is famous for its dazzling stained glass windows (13th - 16th Centuries). The most interesting one is in the fourth chapel in the left-hand aisle. It was made in 1625 by Linard Gontier and represents the "Mystic Press". It shows Christ lying at the foot of the press while the blood gushing from His wound pours into a chalice. A vine bearing the Twelve Apostles is growing out of His chest.

Chaource, which has given its name to a creamy, slightly-matured cheese, lies in the south of Champagne, a humid area that specialises in stock-breeding and dairy products. The Church of St. John the Baptist (*église St-Jean-Baptiste*) houses a statue of the **Laying in the Tomb** carved in 1515 by a sculptor known as the "Master of Sad Faces". The gravity of the facial expressions and folds in the clothing make the statue one of the finest examples of Champagne-style sculpture.

Sens. The central doorway in the cathedral, the first large Gothic building in France (1130 - 1168), includes a superb statue of St. Stephen dressed in a deacon's robes backing onto the central jamb. This is a priceless example of early Gothic statuary.

The former **royal saltworks in Arc-et-Senans** is one of the few examples left of industrial architecture dating from the second half of the 18th Century. The building of this "ideal town", which was commissioned by the King's Council, was entrusted to Nicolas Ledoux. He designed a community with the factory buildings and houses laid out in a circle around the Director's house which has a peristyle with pillars consisting of a succession of alternating square and cylindrical keystones.

Saint-Claude, at the centre of the tourist routes through Jura, owes its fame to the manufacture of pipes, the speciality of the skilful local wood-turners in the late 18th Century. The same know-how led to the creation, c. 1460, of superb **choirstalls** in St. Peter's Cathedral (*cathédrale Saint-Pierre*). A cabinet-maker from Geneva named Jehan de Vitry depicted St. Roman and St. Lupicin, hermits who lived on the site of the present cathedral c. 430 A.D. Their followers founded an abbey which reached the heights of its influence in the 12th Century.

The church in Brou. Brou is a modest suburb of Bourg-en-Bresse but it boasts a very interesting church built in the Late Gothic style and filled with a profusion of decorative features. Margaret of Austria, whose life was one long string of misfortunes, decided in 1506 that she would have a monastery built to ensure eternal rest for the ashes of her deceased husband, Philibert the Fair, in accordance with a vow taken in earlier times by her mother-in-law.

The church was built in just 19 years, under the direction of a master stonemason from Flanders, Loys Van Boghem. The triangular West Front (*opposite, bottom*) has a Renaissance doorway and is very ornate.

The chancel contains the tombs of **Margaret of Bourbon** (*bottom, left*), **Philibert the Handsome** (*middle, left*) and **Margaret of Austria** (*top, left and right*). These tombs represent the most perfect example of Flemish-style carving in Burgundy. **Margaret** is shown both dead and alive, lying on a slab of black marble at the top and laid out in her shroud at the bottom. A canopy covered with a profusion of carvings bears her motto, "*Fortune infortune for one*".

Left: The **Hérisson Falls** are among the most spectacular waterfalls in **Jura**. At the place known as "L'Eventail", the river leaps down a height of 211 ft. in a series of terraces, forming a succession of curtains of water.

Overleaf: The **Baume Corrie** is a gigantic notch carved out of the Jura Plateau by erosion. At the foot of the slopes are rock falls overgrown by grass and shrubs. High cliffs, topped by forest, bar the end of the valley. In the background is Baume-les-Messieurs, whose Benedictine abbey was founded in the 6th Century by St. Columba, the well-known Irish monk. Twelve of his monks left the abbey in 910 A.D. to found Cluny (*p. 75*).

Ronchamp. The chapel of *Notre-Dame-du-Haut* built in 1955 is one of the most important of all contemporary religious buildings. Its designer, Le Corbusier, made maximum use of the flexibility of the building material (concrete) to obtain a piece of architecture that is more akin to sculpture, with curving lines and slopes that never cease to surprise visitors, while at the same time creating a building that blends perfectly into the landscape.

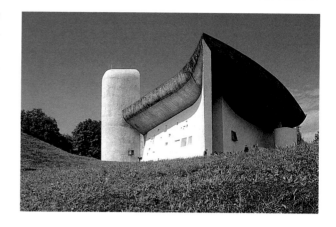

Middle, right: **The Lac Blanc**. In the Vosges Mountains, lakes fill small corries gouged out by glaciers. Situated at an altitude of 3,425 ft. and surrounded by granite cliffs, the Lac Blanc is the deepest of all the lakes in the range (234 ft.).

The **Hillcrest Route** (*Route des Crêtes*) running from the Bonhomme Pass to Thann provides an ideal solution for people wanting to see the **Vosges** at their best. On one side, the view extends as far as the Alsace Plain, while to the other it stretches as far as the mountains covered in their dark mantle of forest and woodland. Towards the summit, the alpine pastures, which are covered in snow throughout the winter months, provide grazing for animals again from May to October.

Colmar. The prosperity of Colmar, in the heart of the Alsace Plain, has been based on the wine trade since the 13th Century. The old town is delightful, with half-timbered houses, carved façades and flower-decked balconies. The R. Lauch flows peacefully between two lines of old houses, forming "**Little Venice**" (*top, left*) which separates the erstwhile tanning district from the Krutenau, once the market garden area.

The Unterlinden Museum is housed in a 13th-century convent. Its chapel contains the famous **Issenheim Reredos** (*top, right*). Painted by Mathias Grünewald between 1512 and 1516, it comprises ten paintings whose overall meaning remains a mystery. The stark contrast between the dark areas and brilliantly-vivid sections, the attitude and bearing of the characters, the symbolism of the animals, and the choice of colours provide a dramatic, spiritual evocation of suffering. One of the panels depicts the Conversation of St. Anthony and St. Paul the Hermit.

Saverne, situated on the eastern slopes of a mountain pass that links the Lorraine Plateau to the Alsace Plain, was the property, from the 13th Century to the French Revolution, of the Prince-Archbishops of Strasburg who welcomed Louis XIV and Louis XV to the town. The castle we see today was commissioned by Cardinal Louis de Rohan. Built of red sandstone after the previous castle had been destroyed by fire in 1779, it has a majestic Louis XVI façade on the north side. The pilastered wings flank a central peristyle comprised of eight Corinthian columns. Louis de Rohan, who led a life of luxury in his palace in Strasburg, was exiled as a result of his involvement in a scandal that wrongfully besmirched the Queen's reputation. When he returned to Strasburg, he refused to take an oath of fidelity to the Revolution, sought refuge across the Rhine, and died in Ettenheim in 1803.

Saint-Dié. Situated in the heart of the Vosges forest, Saint-Dié grew up around a Benedictine monastery founded by St. Déodat in the 7th Century. The old canons' cloisters (15th and 16th Centuries) have superb Flamboyant Gothic bays and ribbed vaulting supported on engaged colonettes and pilasters. The galleries originally connected the parish church and the cathedral.

Riquewihr. Riquewihr belonged to the Dukes of Wurtemburg until the French Revolution and has retained many reminders of the Rhenish Renaissance style. Its 16th and 17th-century red sandstone houses form an attractively uniform village in the midst of the Alsace vineyards which produce the highly-acclaimed Riesling. They benefit from the morning sunshine and the protection afforded by the Vosges against bad weather approaching from the west.

The vineyards of Alsace date back to the 3rd Century A.D. and cover most of the slopes of the foothills of the Vosges. They also cling to the lower slopes of the mountainsides. Production reaches as much as 800,000 hectolitres per year but local winegrowers are concerned to produce quality rather than quantity. This they achieve thanks to meticulous maintenance and constant monitoring.

Strasburg. This erstwhile free imperial city was annexed to France by Louis XIV in 1681. The old Strateburgum (i.e. "the town of roads") has been the seat of the Council of Europe since 1949 and is constantly reinforcing its position in Europe as a centre of excellence for the Arts, intellectual pursuits and politics.

Its cathedral (*top*), built from 1176 onwards, is one of the finest Gothic churches in France. The **radiating West Front** includes ornate carvings. The lower registers of the tympanum (*middle, right*) date from the 13th Century and illustrate the Life of Jesus with a marked sense of realism.

Once the district of tanneries and flour mills, **Little France** (*bottom, right*) is delightful because of its Renaissance houses whose corbelled façades line the banks of the R. Ill.

Perched at an altitude of 2,460 ft, **Haut-Koenigsbourg Castle** boasts a triple row of sandstone walls high above the Alsace Plain. The Hohenstaufens' castle, which was burnt down by the Swedes in 1633 during the Thirty Years' War, was rebuilt in the early years of this century by Kaiser Wilhelm II.

Metz, the former capital of Lotharingia, has been a religious centre since time immemorial (it was the seat of a bishopric in the 3rd Century) and has always been of prime military importance, beacuse of its geographical situation near the Franco-German border.

St. Stephen's Cathedral, built of yellow Jaumont stone, dominates the upper town. The Neo-Gothic West Door was added on in 1903.

Once the capital of the Dukes of Lorraine, **Nancy** still has an outstanding architectural heritage. The **Place Stanislas** is a perfect example of elegance and balance, both of them features of 18th-century France. Stanislas Leszczynski, Louis XV's father-in-law, decided to order to building of a new square in 1752, to link the old town to the new. Close cooperation between the architect, Emmanuel Héré, and Jean Lamour who was a genius as far as wrought ironwork was concerned, has given the square a harmony rarely equalled anywhere else.

The size and variety (13th - 20th Centuries) of the stained glass windows in **Metz Cathedral** have earnt it the nickname "The Good Lord's Lantern". The left transept is suffused in the warm tones of Marc Chagall's *Scenes from Paradise on Earth*.

Rheims Cathedral. Rheims, the town in which France's kings were crowned, has one of the largest Gothic cathedrals in the Christian world, built in the 13th Century. The beautifully-proportioned **West Front** (*top, left*) reaches skywards at every level (doorways, pinnacles, Kings' Gallery and towers). The statue of the **Smiling**

Angel (*top, right*) is characteristic of the style common to the Champagne region, with a lively, expressive face and unrestricted body movement.

The relative narrowness of the **nave** (*opposite*) compared to its length (448 ft.) and a design of elevations in which slenderness and upthrust were the main features give an impressive sensation of height. The arches, supported by massive pillars with capitals decorated with flowers, extend into a blind storey. Above that are the upper windows divided into lancets by a mullion.

Left : The Cloister Museum of **Notre-Dame-en-Vaux** in **Châlons-sur-Marne** contains the sculptures designed as decoration for cloisters discovered in 1960. Dating from the 12th Century, the sculptures clearly show the transition from Romanesque to Gothic, especially in the facial expressions. The capitals depict scenes from the Life of Christ.

The old town of **Laon** perches on a hilltop above a seemingly infinite plain. It was this geographical situation that persuaded the Carolingian monarchs to choose it as their capital in 840 A.D, before Hugh Capet decided on Paris in 987 A.D.

Notre-Dame Cathedral is one of the oldest Gothic buildings in France. The presence of the lantern-tower above the transept crossing is a reminder of the earlier, Romanesque, period. The four towers are surprisingly light despite their mass. They include wide bays flanked by slender turrets.

Opposite : The **vineyards of Champagne** cover an area of 27,000 hectares to each side of the R. Marne south of Rheims, between Bar-sur-Aube and Bar-sur-Seine. Vines were grown here by the Ancient Gauls and the local wines were all naturally sparkling. This led Dom Perignon, cellarer to the Benedictine Abbey of Hautvilliers, to give the wine added sparkle by introducing a system of double fermentation. Nowadays, almost 200,000,000 bottles of champagne are produced annually. The wine is best drunk when it is three or four years old.

Rheims Mountain (*top*) is a rugged limestone plateau. The hillsides are covered with vines that produce the most famous of all the champagnes.

The **Champagne de Castellane** cellars in **Epernay** (*bottom*) cover an area of more than 6 miles. A Museum specialising in the Traditions of Champagne gives an insight into the work of coopers and cellarers.

Set in the heart of **Flanders, Saint-Omer** has a rich religious and aristocratic history, still remembered thanks to its fine Classical mansions and the cathedral (13th - 15th Centuries) best-known for the works of art it contains. The most amazing of them all is **the tomb of Eustace du Croÿ**, Bishop of Saint-Omer. Carved in the 16th Century by Jacques Dubroeucq, it is unusual in that it shows the deceased in prayer, kneeling in front of his own dead body.

When the **basilica in Avioth** comes into view round a bend in a small country road, it is something of a surprise. The church, once a place of pilgrimage, was completed in the early 15th Century and was built in the Flamboyant Gothic style. The South Portal dedicated to the Virgin Mary (the drapes carved in the Champagne style on the base are particularly outstanding) is preceded by a small building known as the "*Recevresse*" where pilgrims used to place their offerings.

The **R. Meuse** twists and turns its way through the Ardennes Forest. **Monthermé**, built on both banks of the river, is an ideal centre for people wishing to tour the surrounding uplands. A path leads to the beauty spot known as The Long Rock (*Longue Roche*) from which the view stretches right over the valley towards the rounded wooded hills of the Ardennes.

Lille, the bustling capital of French Flanders, has taken advantage of its geographical situation to become one of Europe's main cities of the future, lying as it does in the centre of the North-South axis. Yet the city has not forgotten its past and the work undertaken in its historic centre highlights the periods during which it was variously under Flemish, Austrian, Spanish and finally, in the reign of Louis XIV, French rule. The Place du Général-de-Gaulle (or **Grand'Place**) is the centre of life in Lille. The Old Exchange (1652) on the eastern side of the square is a pleasing combination of Louis XIII and Flemish styles.

Amiens, capital of Picardy, is famous for its exceptionally-large cathedral (471 ft. long, 136 ft. high from floor to ceiling), which is in fact the biggest Gothic building in France. It is remarkably uniform in architectural style because the building work was completed in such a short time. Robert de Luzarches had no hesitation in having the stones cut and measured in the quarry so that the workmen could assemble them as soon as they were delivered to the site.

Above the three porches, in the upper gallery, are huge statues of royal personages. Between the towers with their double bays is the large 16th-century rose window built in an elegant Flamboyant Gothic style.

Arras. It passed from the hands of the Counts of Artois in the 12th to 14th Centuries to the Dukes of Burgundy before becoming a Spanish possession from 1492 to 1640. Around its two main squares (**Grand'Place** and Place des Héros) are unique examples of 17th and 18th-century man-

sions. Built in the Flemish style, they are topped by Dutch gables and curved pediments. On the ground floor are arcades built to protect the traders and market stallholders in inclement weather.

A large market is held every Saturday on the two squares.

Opposite: **The Opal Coast** consists of the edge of a limestone plateau which has been eroded by the sea. Its headlands recede by approximately 83 ft. every year. Between Boulogne and Calais, the chalk cliffs face out towards the English coast less than 20 miles away. From **Cap Blanc-Nez** which rises to a height of 471 ft. the view extends as far as **Cap Gris-Nez**, the headland that marks the boundary between the English Channel and the North Sea. The underground offices of the CROSS (the Regional Centre for Assistance and Rescue at Sea) keep watch over some of the busiest shipping lanes in the world.

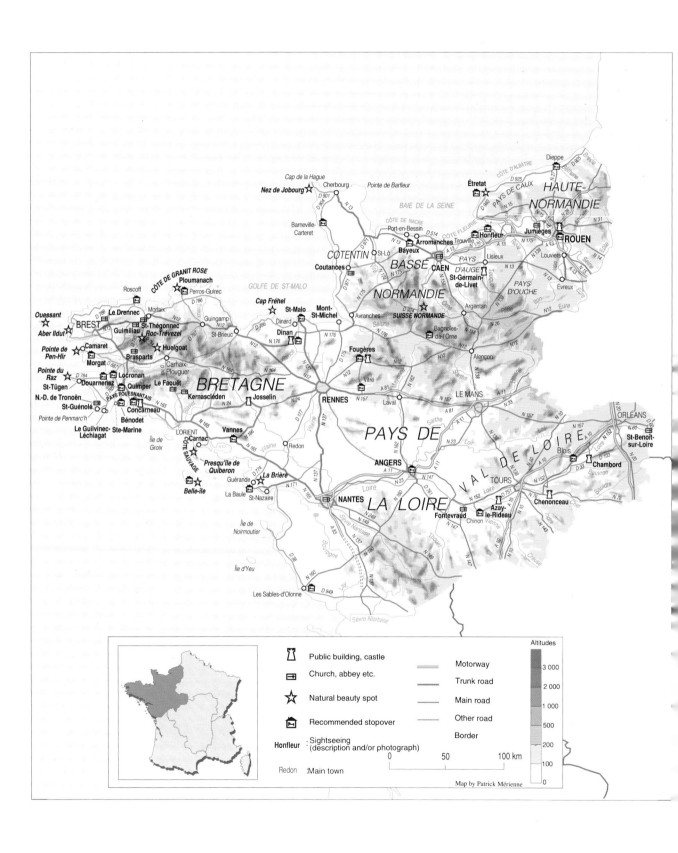

Cap de la Hague
Nez de Jobourg   Cherbourg   Pointe de Barfleur   Dieppe
                                                                    CÔTE D'ALBÂTRE   D 925
                                                                                    PAYS DE CAUX   HAUTE-
                                                            Étretat   NORMANDIE
                                                                                                     ROUEN
                                                BAIE DE LA SEINE
                                    CÔTE DE NACRE   Jumièges
Barneville-   Port-en-Bessin   Honfleur   Louviers
Carteret   Arromanches   Trouville   CÔTE FLEURIE
                        St-Lô   Bayeux   PAYS
COTENTIN   Coutances   CAEN   D'AUGE   Lisieux   Evreux
                                            BASSE   St-Germain-   PAYS
                                            NORMANDIE   de-Livet   D'OUCHE
Roscoff   CÔTE DE GRANIT ROSE
                    Ploumanach   SUISSE NORMANDE   Argentan
                    Perros-Guirec   GOLFE DE ST-MALO
                Morlaix   Cap Fréhel   St-Malo   Mont-   Bagnoles-
Le Drennec   Guingamp   Dinard   St-Michel   Avranches   de-l'Orne   Alençon
Ouessant   BREST   St-Thégonnec   St-Brieuc   Dinan
Aber Ildut   Guimiliau Roc-Trévezel
Camaret   Brasparts   Huelgoat   Fougères
Pointe de   Carhaix-   LE MANS
Pen-Hir   Morgat   Locronan Plouguer   Vitré
Pointe du   Douarnenez Quimper   Le Faouët   BRETAGNE
Raz   Laval
St-Tügen   PAYS BIGOUDEN   Kernascléden   RENNES
N.-D. de Tronoën   Concarneau   Josselin
St-Guénolé   PAYS DE
Pointe de Penmarc'h   Bénodet   ORLÉANS
Le Guilvinec-   Ste-Marine   LA LOIRE
Léchiagat   LORIENT   Vannes   Blois   St-Benoît-
                    Carnac   sur-Loire
            Île de   Redon   ANGERS   TOURS   Chambord
            Groix   CÔTE SAUVAGE   PAYS DE   Chenonceau
            Presqu'île de   LA LOIRE   Azay-
            Quiberon   Guérande   La Brière   NANTES   le-Rideau
            Belle-Île   La Baule   St-Nazaire   Fontevraud   Chinon
                    Île de
                    Noirmoutier

                    Île d'Yeu

                    Les Sables-d'Olonne

Altitudes

	3 000
	2 000
	1 000
	500
	200
	100
	0

Public building, castle   Motorway
Church, abbey etc.   Trunk road
Natural beauty spot   Main road
Recommended stopover   Other road
                               Border
Honfleur :Sightseeing
         (description and/or photograph)
                               0   50   100 km
Redon :Main town

Map by Patrick Mérienne

NORTH-WESTERN FRANCE

Normandy, Brittany, Loire Valley

Brasparts (Finistère) : The pietà on the calvary.

Chenonceau.

Upper Normandy is split in half by the Seine Valley. To the north of the river is the **Caux Region**, a chalky plateau lined by tall cliffs. To the south is the **Ouche Region**, an area of forest and pasture that constitutes a transitional belt leading into the rich meadows of the **Auge Region**, the undulating region famous for its cheeses (camembert, livarot, pont-l'évêque) and its cider. The **Floral Coast** attracts visitors because of its fine sandy beaches, its prestigious seaside resorts (Deauville, Cabourg) and its bustling fishing harbours.

Lower Normandy covers the Caen Plain, a major farming area bordered to the north by an almost straight stretch of coastline, and the **Cherbourg Peninsula**, the northern section of the Armorican landmass where the gently-rolling countryside is divided into checkerboard squares by the meadows and hedgerows. The west coast is particularly varied, with granite cliffs, sand dunes and sandy beaches leading down to **Mont Saint-Michel Bay**.

The picture that immediately springs to mind when **Brittany** is mentioned is one of a coastal region (the Armor) with 808 miles of headlands, coves and creeks providing shelter for the fishing harbours and a string of tiny islands exposed to the wrath of the ocean waves. The interior (the Argoat) is partly covered with moorland and forest and has retained many memories, carved in granite, of a religious faith that is still very much alive today.

The **Loire Valley** can be considered as the supreme example of the French countryside and way of life. Its mild climate, delightful scenery, and countless castles that began life as a means of defence against attack in the Middle Ages before being turned into homes for the sovereigns of France, inspired writers who brought the French language its reputation. Among them were Ronsard and du Bellay, founders of the Pléiade school in the 16th Century.

Downstream from Rouen is **Jumièges Abbey** which fully deserved the praise of archaeologist Robert de Lasteyrie ("One of the most admirable ruins anywhere in France") given the inherent grandeur in the remains of its buildings and the elegance of its natural surroundings. Founded in the 7th Century by St. Philibert, this major mediaeval monastery in Normandy was destroyed as a result of the Viking invasions. The abbey was rebuilt in the 10th Century by Duke William Long-Sword. Sold off at public auction in 1793, it served as a source of building stone until, in 1853, its new owner decided to save the last remaining ruins for posterity.

Rouen, a large river and seaport, still has a large number of interesting historic buildings. The "Golden Age" of the capital of Normandy (mid 15th - early 16th Centuries) was a period of prosperity when the merchants of Rouen contracted with shipowners to travel the new sea routes and sell their products. It was at this time that the Law Courts were built, a superb Renaissance building whose design concepts are evident on the frontage. The lower storey is austere but the decorative features become increasingly ornate further up the building until, at balustrade level, it becomes a veritable piece of lacework in stone.

Bottom : Beyond the heavy gate stands **Saint-Germain-de-Livet**, a delightful little country house hiding away in the middle of Normandy's meadows and pastures. The 16th-century residence has checkerboard bonding made of stone and coloured brick.

Top: **Honfleur**, and its old basin lined with tall, narrow, slate-hung houses, has inspired countless artists and poets. Situated at the mouth of the R. Seine, the small town played an active part in the maritime expeditions of days gone by. One of its sons, Jean Denis, was the first person to sail up the St. Lawrence Seaway in 1506.

Honfleur was the birthplace of humorist Alphonse Allaire and composer Erik Satie. Baudelaire wrote his *Invitation to a Voyage* here while staying at his mother's house, and the artists Boudin, Daubigny and Corot all set up their easels in the locality.

Overleaf: The **cliffs at Etretat**. The elegant resort of Etretat is flanked by spectacular chalk cliffs. The archway known as the *Porte d'Aval* (Downstream Gate) stretches out to the 227-foot *Aiguille* (Needle) made famous by Arsène Lupin, the hero of a novel by Maurice Leblanc called *L'Aiguille creuse*. Etretat has an attractive shingle beach with a promenade running along its entire length.

Photo by courtesy of Bayeux Town Council.

Bottom: The tiny seaside resort of **Arromanches** was the place selected by the Allies as the site of the gigantic Mulberry harbour that was such a vital feature of the D-Day Landings in 1944 on the Normandy coast. 146 concrete blocks 227 ft. long were sunk in the roadstead so that 33 jetties and 10 miles of floating roadway could be set up.

Bottom: The **Orne Valley** has acquired the nickname of the "Norman Alps" because of the few rocky escarpments that jut up above the countryside. The most attractive area lies between Putanges-Pont-Ecrepin and Thury-Harcourt, to the south of Caen.

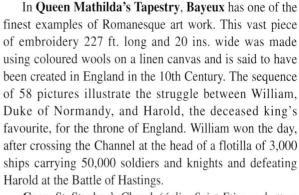

In **Queen Mathilda's Tapestry**, **Bayeux** has one of the finest examples of Romanesque art work. This vast piece of embroidery 227 ft. long and 20 ins. wide was made using coloured wools on a linen canvas and is said to have been created in England in the 10th Century. The sequence of 58 pictures illustrate the struggle between William, Duke of Normandy, and Harold, the deceased king's favourite, for the throne of England. William won the day, after crossing the Channel at the head of a flotilla of 3,000 ships carrying 50,000 soldiers and knights and defeating Harold at the Battle of Hastings.

Caen. St. Stephen's Church (*église Saint-Etienne, bottom left*) is part of the **Men's Abbey** (*abbaye aux Hommes*) founded by William the Conqueror in 1066 as a penitence after the papacy lifted the excommunication that had been pronounced after his marriage to his distant cousin, Mathilda. (The Ladies' Abbey in the eastern part of the town dates from the same period and was built for the same reason.) The austere West Front, nothing more than a gable wall without any portals or rose window, surprises those who see it for the first time because of the superb upthrust of its towers rising to traceried spires dating from the 13th Century.

The spires on the **Ladies' Abbey** (*bottom, right*) founded by Queen Mathilda were replaced in the early years of the 18th Century by heavy balustrades.

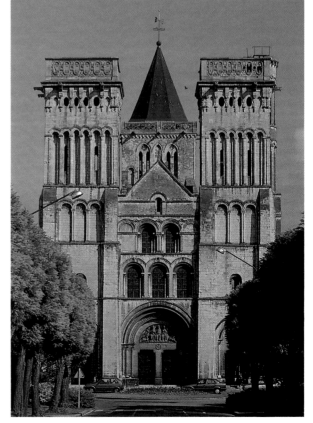

To the north-west of the Cherbourg Peninsula is the **Nez de Jobourg**, a sheer headland surrounded by reefs. In the foreground is Sennival Cove. The western coast of the Peninsula closes off the horizon with its endless beaches of fine sand.

In the heart of the Cherbourg Peninsula lies **Coutances**, dominated by the mass of its cathedral, a superb example of Norman Gothic architecture at its very best. The same Norman architecture can be seen in the magnificent octagonal **lantern tower**, a veritable well of light 133 ft. above the transept crossing. This daring piece of building, which includes a triforium, is supported on a series of overhangs.

situated below the upper town. It still has its mediaeval walls and thirteen towers.

Bottom: **Rennes**. Once the capital of the Duchy of Brittany, then capital of the province after its annexation to France following the marriage of Anne of Brittany and Charles VIII in 1491, Rennes was devastated by a huge fire in 1720. The districts that disappeared in the flames were replaced by a network of streets laid out at right angles to each other and by granite buildings, all of them built to plans drawn up by Jacques Gabriel who also designed the Town Hall (*left*). The frontage of the Law Courts (*Palais de Justice*) in the background dates from an earlier period than the redevelopment of the town centre, having been designed by Salomon de Brosse in 1618. Its austerity is a forerunner of Classical taste and it blends perfectly into the monumental setting of 17th and 18th-century houses. The theatre opposite the Town Hall was built in 1832.

Top: **Fougères**. This old fortified town was an outpost of the Duchy of Brittany until the end of the 15th Century, in the days when Brittany stood up to the power of the Capetian monarchs of France. The castle is rather strangely

An unusual setting, a history dating back some one thousand years, and a style of architecture that is as beautiful as it is daring have combined to give **Mont Saint-Michel** the nickname of "Marvel of the Western World".

In the 8th Century after Michael, the Archangel had appeared to the monastery's founder, a modest chapel was built on a tiny, isolated granite island in an immense bay whose waters recede twice a day thanks to the movements of a tide with a huge amplitude. It was followed by a Carolingian abbey under Benedictine Rule then, until the 16th Century, by Romanesque and Gothic buildings. Because space was at a premium on the rock, the buildings had to be built one above the other. They are topped by the church, cloisters, and refectory (*opposite*).

The Gothic **cloisters** (*bottom*) high above the Bay that can be seen from the West gallery have staggered rows of slender pink granite colonettes. The squinches are decorated with delicately carved foliage and plants.

The **Knights' Chamber** (*bottom*) was the monks' work room heated by fires lit in the vast hearths. It was here that they copied and illuminated manuscripts.

Opposite, top: **Saint-Malo** gained wealth and prosperity from the 16th Century onwards thanks to trade in furs from Canada and cod-fishing off the Grand Banks. It owes its fame to Duguay-Trouin (1673-1736) and Surcouf (1773-1827), brave buccaneers who tirelessly hunted down English ships.

Opposite, bottom: The rocks at **Cap Fréhel** stand some 227 ft. above the sea below. Lashed by the wind and waves, they are the natural habitat of huge colonies of cormorants and gulls. To the east is the outline of the Fort La Latte peninsula. The fortress, now restored, has retained its feudal appearance.

Bottom: **The Pink Granite Coast**. The piles of pink rocks in Ploumanac'h have acquired strange shapes. A walk along the coastal footpath from the *Château du Diable* to the beach in Saint-Guirec gives people an opportunity to try and recognise, amidst all the granite boulders shaped by centuries of erosion, the ones known as the "rabbit", the "tortoise", the "mushroom" etc.

Top: **Dinan**. The small Breton town owes its fame to Bertrand Du Guesclin who entered the king's service in 1356. His victorious campaigns against the English won him the title of King of Grenada and Constable of France. The old town still has many of its half-timbered houses, some of them built over arcades.

The **parish closes** are an unusual manifestation of Breton faith and art work. Erected in the second half of the 16th Century, they were part of the campaign to bring a deeper sense of Christianity to rural districts by giving greater popularity to the worship of the Apostles and Saints.

The funeral chapel, or ossuary, in **Saint-Thégonnec** (*top*) bears witness to the never-ending popularity of Renaissance motifs in decorative work. The finely-carved frontage serves as a reminder that prayers to the deceased were a major feature of faith in Brittany.

The calvary in **Guimiliau** (*bottom*) includes more than 200 statues whose expressive features (in the illustration of the Washing of the Feet, note the faces with eyes closed) show a profound sense of theatricality and movement.

Top: The **abers**, or rias, on the north-west coast of Finistère are the estuaries of small rivers along which the seawater flows at high tide. The juxtaposition of sea-based activities and Breton countryside is a picturesque sight, especially in Port-Lanildut.

Bottom: The rocks in **Le Huelgoat** form one of the strangest sights in inland Brittany. With the neighbouring forest, they are a popular place for excursions and their names are highly evocative e.g. Devil's Cave, Mill Rocks, Boars' Lake etc.

Bottom: **Fishing** is one of the traditional trades in Brittany whether along the 932 miles of coastline (inshore fishery), in the area from the Bay of Biscay to Iceland (deep-sea fishing), or on the Grand Banks off Newfoundland and up to Greenland (high-sea fishery). On land are canning factories and shipyards like the ones in **Lechiagat** opposite Le Guilvinec, all of them linked to this trade and to the complementary sector of shellfish and oyster or mussel farming.

Top: **The island of Ushant** off the coast of Finistère is much feared by seafarers because of the mist, the jagged reefs, and the strength of the current, all of which have caused many a shipwreck. To the north-west of the island, the shoreline consists of rocky headlands battered by the waves - a wild, yet beautiful sight.

Opposite, top: The **Pointe de Penhir** extends into isolated rocks known as the Tas de Pois (literally "pile of peas"), forming one of the most impressive beauty spots in the **Crozon Peninsula**. The deeply-gashed cliffs have been shaped by the erosion of the waves which has worn away the sandstone and left behind seams of harder quartzite.

Opposite, bottom: **Camaret-sur-Mer** on the north coast of the **Crozon Peninsula** is a busy lobster-fishing port and a seaside resort much appreciated for its bracing climate. Its geographical location opposite Brest Harbour led it to be attacked on several occasions. It was fortified by Vauban in 1689 and, in 1694, it successfully repulsed an attack by a huge Anglo-Dutch fleet.

Bottom, left: The **Roc Trévezel** is the highest peak (alt. 1,248 ft.) in the Monts d'Arrée. From the rocky scarp, there is a vast panoramic view of the Breton "mountains" which deserve their title despite their low altitude because of their austerity and climate.

The **Pointe du Raz** forms the tip of Cap Sizun and, with the Penmarc'h Peninsula, it constitutes the coastline of the Cornouaille area. Its dark mass of rock pitted with caves stands to one side of the very dangerous race where the currents are unusually strong and the reefs numerous. To the other side of this stretch of water lies the island of Sein, which can just be seen on the horizon. On the outermost tiny rocky islet is the Vieille lighthouse.

Next to the chapel of **Our Lady of Tronoën** in the middle of the sand dunes on the edge of Audierne Bay is the oldest calvary in Brittany (1450). Carved in a soft granite and nearly overrun with lichen, it tells the story of the Childhood and Passion of Christ. The chapel has a slender traceried belfry and stone vaulting, an unusual sight in Brittany.

Saint-Tügen. The religious processions known as *pardons* bear witness to the strength of religious feeling in Brittany. Banners and statues of saints are carried across the countryside by lines of believers singing hymns. Pierre Jakez Hélias in his book *The Horse of Pride* described the intensity of feeling at religious processions such as these. "There are certain places of worship that instil such fervour that even atheists cannot fail to be impressed."

The headdresses are the most unusual feature of the traditional Breton costume. Few wear them today except for the older women, and then mainly in the Cornouaille area. The **Bigouden headdress** is a tall cylindrical piece of lace and is undoubtedly the strangest of them all.

Top: **Saint-Guénolé**. From the Eckmühl Lighthouse with its range of 34 miles, the view extends beyond the Chapel of Our Lady of Joy, and the beach and village of Saint-Guénolé, to Audierne Bay and the coastline of the Cornouaille area. This is a typical example of Breton scenery.

Left: **Le Guilvinec**. Even the most modern fishing techniques have not destroyed the age-old skills such as the repairing of fishing nets by hand.

Opposite: Clinging onto the hillside is **Locronan**, which still has reminders of its prosperous past based, from the 16th to 18th Centuries, on the canvas trade. Made from hemp grown in the Cornouaille area, the town supplied sailcloth for the ships of Brittany, England and Spain. Indeed, its products were sold as far afield as the Americas. The Place de l'Eglise centres on a well. Around it are the weavers' and merchants' houses. The 15th-century church, with its robust square belfry, has a

very interesting **pulpit** (1707) on which the carved panels tell the life story of St. Ronan, a preacher traditionally said to have come from Ireland in the 5th Century. The craftsmen of Locronan still perpetuate the art of woodcarving and weaving.

The **Fouesnant area** has a large number of churches, chapels and calvaries. The chapel in **Le Drennec**, not far from Bénodet, has a huge fountain in front of it (16th Century). In a Gothic niche is a granite Pietà.

The **Odet Estuary** in the heart of an area of trees and meadows is a natural mooring that is very popular with yachtsmen. **Bénodet** on the left bank and **Sainte-Marine** on the right bank both have yachting marinas and superb fine sandy beaches.

Top, left: Life in **Concarneau**, the second-largest fishing harbour in France, revolves around the arrival and departure of its trawler fleet and the opening of the fish auction. The **Walled Town** forms a small island surrounded by thick walls built in the 14th Century and designed to protect the citadel during the days of feudal warfare. The entrance consists of two bridges separated by a fortified forework. *Middle left*, the fishing harbour in Concarneau.

Top, right: At the head of the Odet Estuary lies **Quimper**, once the capital of the Cornouaille area and still the most typically Breton of all the large towns in north-western France. The **Rue Kéréon** lined with old corbelled houses leads to the cathedral whose spires built in 1856 rise proudly heavenwards.

Left: **Kernascléden**. The church in this quiet village in inland Brittany is famous for its late 15th-century **frescoes**. The artists let their enthusiasm and imagination run riot when they illustrated all the tortures of Hell in the south arm of the transept.

Josselin. The Rohan family seat was destroyed on several occasions, in particular in the period following the War of Breton Succession that, in the 14th Century, opposed Jeanne de Penthièvre supported by the Valois camp to Jean de Montfort. The castle still has its tall towers high above the R. Oust. Between them, forming a strange contrast, are the windows of the palace built overlooking the courtyard in the 16th Century.

The **Chapel of Saint-Fiacre-du-Faouët** was built in 1450 by the Boutevilles, rivals of the Rohans who had commissioned the church in Kernascléden (*opposite*). The painted wooden **rood screen** is a masterpiece of Flamboyant Gothic art. On the side facing the nave, it includes scenes from the Annunciation, the Temptation of Adam and Eve and the Crucifixion.

Vannes, which was the capital of the Venetii, one of the most powerful tribes in Ancient Gaul, lies at the tip of the Morbihan Gulf. In the 9th Century, Nominoë, who was named Duke of Vannes by Charlemagne and, in 826 A.D., Duke of Brittany by Louis the Pious, acquired authority over all the Bretons. Vannes was the capital of this new kingdom but it was to be downgraded to a mere duchy one century later.

In front of the town walls are the old wash-houses with picturesque slate roofs.

The **Quiberon Peninsula** was once an island but it became linked to the mainland by a build-up of alluvium. Its west coast, better-known as the **Wild Coast**, is a succession of jagged cliffs, rocks and reefs. The crashing rollers and undercurrents make the small beaches dotted along the coastline unsuitable for bathing.

The **Carnac alignments** consist of almost 2,800 standing stones set out in parallel lines. They are the silent witnesses of the megalithic civilisation which flourished in Brittany during the Stone Age (4,670 - 2,000 B.C.). During this period, man became sedentary. He began to farm and raise livestock, produce polished artefacts, make pottery, and erect these monuments whose purpose still remains a mystery.

Belle-Ile off the coast of the Quiberon Peninsula is a vast schist plateau with deeply gashed edges. The island is, in fact, a piece of the ancient Breton shoreline which collapsed between the island of Yeu and the Cornouaille area. When the glaciers melted 8,000 years ago, they caused a rise in the sea level which separated Belle-Ile from the mainland.

Nantes. The former seat of the Dukes of Brittany is now the capital of the Lower Loire Valley region. Lying at the spot where the R. Loire flows into the sea, Nantes was ideally situated to trade with Lower Brittany, the Poitou area, and far-distant countries. In the 17th and 18th Centuries, the town became extremely prosperous thanks to the "triangular trade" - slaves bought on the Guinea coast were exchanged for sugar cane in the West Indies. The sugar was then shipped back to Nantes and refined.

The **castle of the Dukes of Brittany**, protected on the outside by huge towers and flanked by a moat, has a more elegant appearance from the courtyard. Building began on the Grand Apartments topped by five tall dormer windows during the reign of François II at the end of the 15th Century and was completed by his daughter, Anne of Brittany. The Golden Crown Tower has Italianate loggias.

The **Brière Regional Country Park** to the north of the Loire Estuary ensures the preservation of a vast area of marshland that has been drained thanks to the single-minded work of man. Over the last five centuries, the local people earned their living from peat, an excellent fertiliser, and from the cutting of reeds. A network of canals leads deep into the heart of the marshes.

The **Apocalypse Tapestry**. Hung in one of the buildings within the walls of **Angers Castle**, this huge tapestry measuring 439 ft. by 16 ft. is both the oldest and the largest still in existence. It was woven by Nicolas Bataille in a Parisian workshop between 1373 and 1383 for Duke Louis I of Anjou. The 76 sequences are remarkable for the purity of the design and the rigorous layout of the composition illustrating the Book of Revelations written by St. John (it describes the victory of Christ and the triumph of the Christian church).

Azay-le-Rideau. Surrounded by water and trees on all sides, this stately home built between 1518 and 1527 for the financier Gilles Berthelot and confiscated after his flight by François I is indisputably the most elegant of all the Loire Valley castles. Its system of defence (corner turrets and parapet walkway) is purely decorative and was designed to underline the social standing of the castle owner.

Fontevraud Abbey was founded in 1101 by Robert d'Arbrissel who had been ordered by the Pope to preach throughout Western France. The Order, which included both contemplative nuns and priests and monks, was under the control and authority of an abbess bearing the title of "chief and general". Despite several periods of more lax discipline, Fontevraud's spiritual and cultural influence survived the centuries until the outbreak of the French Revolution.

The **minster** (*top, left*) was built between 1104 and 1150. It has a wide domed nave reminiscent of the Romanesque architecture of south-western France. In front of the luminous, elegant chancel are the polychrome tombs of the Plantagenets who chose the abbey as their burial ground in 1204 (*Bottom, left : Eleanor of Aquitaine and her husband Henry II, King of England*).

The **kitchens** (*top, left*) have an Anjou-style roof of stones cut into dimaond shapes.

Overleaf: **Chambord**. At the beginning of the Renaissance period, castles lost the strategic purpose that they had had since the Early Middle Ages. They were no longer built on hilltops but instead were set in the middle of attractive countryside, near a river or game-filled forest. Chambord, built for François I from 1519 onwards, is the largest of the Loire Valley castles (507 ft. long and 380 ft. wide). It is an example of perfect architectural and decorative unity and has 440 rooms served by 83 stair-cases. Its frontage is reflected in the waters of the R. Cosson, whose natural course was altered so that it flowed through the park.

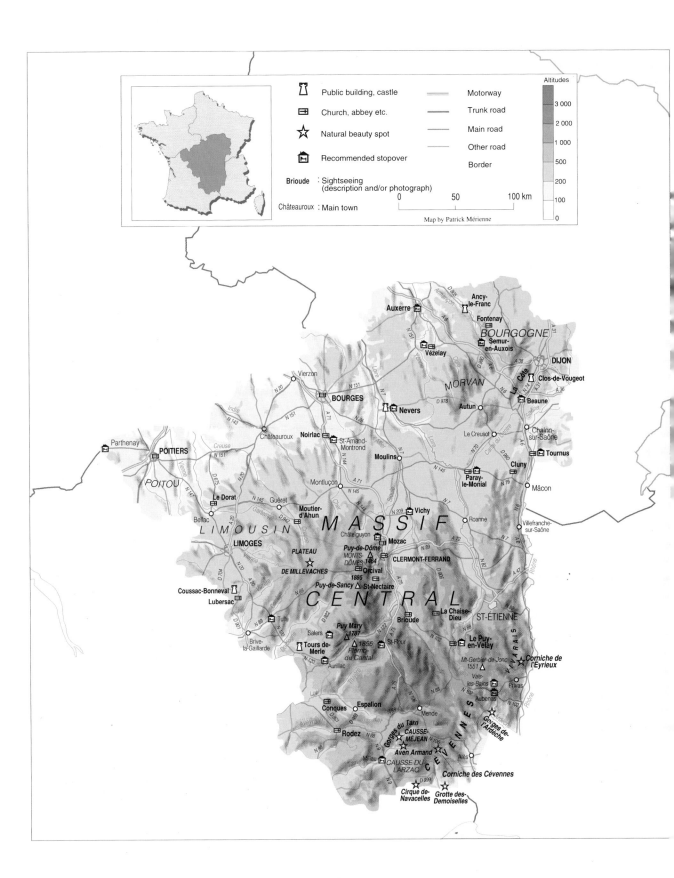

Public building, castle
Church, abbey etc.
Natural beauty spot
Recommended stopover

Motorway
Trunk road
Main road
Other road
Border

Altitudes
3 000
2 000
1 000
500
200
100
0

Brioude : Sightseeing
(description and/or photograph)

Châteauroux : Main town

0   50   100 km

Map by Patrick Mérienne

Auxerre
Ancy-le-Franc
Fontenay
BOURGOGNE
Semur-en-Auxois
Vézelay
MORVAN
La Côte
DIJON
Clos-de-Vougeot
Vierzon
BOURGES
Beaune
Nevers
Autun
Châteauroux
Noirlac
St-Amand-Montrond
Le Creusot
Chalon-sur-Saône
Parthenay
POITIERS
Moulins
Tournus
POITOU
Cluny
Montluçon
Paray-le-Monial
Le Dorat
Guéret
Moutier-d'Ahun
MASSIF
Mâcon
Bellac
LIMOUSIN
Châtelguyon
Vichy
Roanne
Villefranche-sur-Saône
LIMOGES
PLATEAU
DE MILLEVACHES
Puy-de-Dôme
Mozac
MONTS
DÔMES 1464
Orcival
CLERMONT-FERRAND
1885
Coussac-Bonneval
Puy-de-Sancy
St-Nectaire
Lubersac
CENTRAL
La Chaise-Dieu
ST-ÉTIENNE
Brioude
Tulle
Puy Mary
1787
Le Puy-en-Velay
Salers
1855
Plomb-
du Cantal
St-Flour
VIVARAIS
Brive-la-Gaillarde
Tours de-
Merle
Corniche de
l'Eyrieux
Aurillac
Mt-Gerbier-de-Jonc
1551
Vals-
les-Bains
Privas
Aubenas
Conques
Espalion
Mende
Gorges de-
l'Ardèche
Rodez
Gorges du Tarn
CAUSSE-
MÉJEAN
CÉVENNES
Aven Armand
Millau
CAUSSE DU
LARZAC
Alès
Corniche des Cévennes
Cirque de-
Navacelles
Grotte des-
Demoiselles

CENTRAL FRANCE

Burgundy, Massif Central, Limousin, Poitou

The volcanic landscape in the **Sancy Range.**

Beaune : The roofs of the hospice.

Burgundy is famous for its eventful history, under the reign of the dynasty of the Great Valois Dukes (1364-1477), and for the prestigious vineyards covering the **Hillside** (*"Côtes"*), the edge of the "Mountain" overlooking the Saône Plain. To the west are the uplands of the **Morvan**, a fairly isolated area with widely-scattered habitation. The main features of the landscape are the forests on the hilltops and the pastures on the lower slopes.

The volcanic ranges of the Auvergne form the backbone of the **Massif Central**. From south to north, the **Cantal** (Plomb du Cantal, alt. 6,038 ft), **Monts-Dores** (Puy-de-Sancy, alt. 6,130 ft), and **Monts-Dômes** (Puy-de-Dôme, alt. 4,755 ft) make up a strange landscape of conical hills, some of them eroded, and lakes in places where the valleys have been closed off by lava flows. The slopes have alternating stretches of forest and lush pasture where the Salers graze, a robust breed of flame-coloured cattle. The multiplicity of high-quality mineral springs (producing

one-third of French output of bottled water) and thermal springs (with temperatures above 35° C) has led to the setting up of countless spas.

The southern edges of the Massif Central consist of vast plateaux at fairly high altitudes. They are the **Causses** (Larzac, Méjean) gashed in places by deep gorges (Tarn, Ardèche).

The **Limousin** uplands to the west (Millevaches Plateau) are a stony landscape swept by strong winds and lashed by rain. The difficult environment explains the low population density.

The **Poitou** is a plain drained by the affluents of the R. Loire. In some places, there is moorland where flocks of sheep graze; in others, the fields and meadows bear witness to a prosperous farming area specialising in cattle breeding (Charolaises and Limousines which produce high-quality milk) and extensive crop farming (cereals, fodder crops).

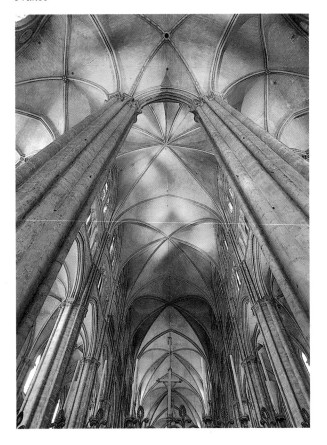

Top: **Bourges. St. Stephen's Cathedral** (*cathédrale Saint-Etienne*, 1200-1270) was the first cathedral to be built south of the Loire and was designed to underline royal authority in the face of the southern provinces that were under English rule. It combines the most sophisticated of all the techniques used in Gothic architecture to distribute and direct thrust. The uniformity of layout and the volume resulting from this technical excellence are an illustration of St. Bernard's statement, "What is God? He is length, width, height, and depth."

Anybody standing at the end of the building between the last two pillars cannot but be filled with a sense of awe at the immense vertical upthrust of the chancel, whose vaulted roof lies 120 ft. above floor level.

The **stained glass windows** in the chancel are, with the ones in Chartres whose technique was copied here in Bourges, some of the most interesting in France. Created in the early 13th Century, they make extensive use of blues and reds. In the Holy Cross Chapel is an illustration of the life of St. Nicholas.

Bottom: The Cistercian abbey in **Noirlac**, in the Cher Valley, is the most complete and best-preserved

Benedictine monastery in France. Founded c. 1130 by Robert of Clairvaux, St. Bernard's cousin, its early years were fraught with difficulties until it received a large donation that allowed it to prosper and develop.

In the centre of the monastery buildings are the multi-foiled Gothic cloisters dating from the late 13th Century. They have slender colonnettes and capitals decorated with plants.

Top: **Fontenay Abbey**, founded in 1118, represents the principles of a monastic existence based on asceticism and hard work, in accordance with the precepts of St. Bernard and the Rule of St. Benedict and in stark contrast to the wealth and power of Cluny (*p. 74*). The **West Front** (*left*), which is totally devoid of any decorative feature, is a perfect expression of this determination. It has seven openings symbolising the Holy Sacraments of the Church. The **chapter house** (*right*) leading into the cloisters has superb quadripartite vaulting. The capitals on the pillars are decorated with acanthus leaves.

Bottom: **Ancy-le-Franc** is a fine example of Classical Renaissance architecture in Burgundy. It was designed by an Italian named Sebastian Serlio, courtier to François I, and consists of four identical façades linked by corner pavilions. The relative austerity of the exterior contrasts sharply with the opulence of the decoration inside the stately home.

Bottom: The old town of **Auxerre**, capital of Lower Burgundy, stretches out along the banks of the R. Yonne, in the shadow of **St. Stephen's Cathedral** (*caéthdrale Saint-Etienne*) built from the 13th to 16th Centuries. The town, which lies at the mouth of the Nevers Canal, has a large marina.

The **vineyards of Burgundy** cover an area of 37,500 hectares on the hillside between Dijon and Chagny south of Beaune and produce the most famous wines in the world with prestigious names such as Gevrey-Chambertin, Clos de Vougeot, Vosne-Romanée, Nuits-Saint-Geogres, Aloxe-Corton, Pommard etc. The **Château du Clos de Vougeot** Estate (*top*) belongs to the Brotherhood of Wine-Tasters which meets once a year to enroll new members. The brotherhood works to promote the wines of Burgundy and France.

Dijon. The former capital of the Dukes of Burgundy enjoyed a long period of prosperity during the reign of the Valois dynasty (1364-1477). While the rich upper middle classes were commissioning the building of comfortable mansions, the "Grand Dukes of the Western World" (Philip the Bold, John the Fearless, Philip the Good and Charles the Brave) were adorning the town with prestigious public

Semur-en-Auxois is set in a delightful spot in the middle of a rich farming area. Notre-Dame Church juts up above the roofs of the old town. The Orle Tower to the right used to control the entrance to the town in the 14th Century, when Semur was the best-protected fortress in the Duchy of Burgundy.

buildings. From the Philip the Good Tower high above the Palace of the Dukes and States of Burgundy, the view extends right over the town. **Notre-Dame Church**, an elegant Gothic building, presented the architect with a number of difficulties because of the lack of space. The **Vogüé Residence** next to the church is roofed with varnished tiles and is one of the first mansions in Dijon to have belonged to a member of the high judicial Court (early 17th Century).

Beaune is both the capital of Burgundy's vineyards and a town of special architectural and artistic interest with a rich heritage. Its **Hospice** (*Hôtel-Dieu, p. 69*), which was founded in 1443 to cater for the sick and afflicted, was designed in the Flemish style in the days when Burgundy's major towns included Lille, Bruges, Ghent and The Hague. The **Last Judgement Polyptych** painted by Roger van der Weyden used to be hung above the altar in the "Grand Chamber of the Poor". The perfection of his work down to the very last detail makes it one of the finest surviving examples of Gothic painting.

Cluny Abbey, founded in the 10th Century by Duke William the Pious of Aquitaine, was the driving force behind the extraordinary spread of the Benedictine Rule in mediaeval Europe. At the beginning of the 12th Century, the Cluniac Order had 1,450 communities and more than 10,000 monks. From the artistic point of view, Cluny is a vital feature of the history of Romanesque sculpture and carving in Burgundy. The "Master of Cluny" whose background remains a mystery since his style broke through suddenly, without any gradual build-up, was the founder of a form which combined movement and suppleness and he used the actions and events of everyday life to represent the most complex religious symbols and themes. The **capitals in the chancel** of Cluny Church, which are displayed in the grain store, have figures set out "against a deep-set background which creates shadows that accentuate their plastic beauty" (Alain Erlande-Brandenburg). The one shown in this photograph represents Hope, in the form of a person firmly grasping a sceptre.

Opposite, bottom: The **Temptation of Eve** displayed in the **Rolin Museum in Autun** was painted by Gislebert who had very probably been trained in the workshops in Vézelay and Cluny. Eve, shown advancing across the ground as if she were swimming in water, is arguably the most feminine and sensual of all figures in Romanesque iconography because of the combined curves of her body and the surrounding plants.

Top: **Vézelay. The Basilica of St. Mary Magdalen** was built between 1096 and 1104 for the pilgrims who came to pray to the relics of Lazarus' sister. It has a narthex in which a carving shows Christ sending his Apostles out as missionaires. The Master of Cluny has created the most skilful and lifelike piece of Burgundian Romanesque sculpture here. The gigantic figure of Christ stands, on long legs, above strange terrestrial beings while the impetuous wind of the spirit blows out the clothes like the sails of a ship.

The capitals in the nave (*p. 5*) carved by anonymous artists show exceptional mastery of composition and movement.

Opposite, top, left: **Moulins. The Triptych painted by the Master of Moulins** (1498) in the cathedral is one of the last gems of Gothic painting. The central panel, showing the Virgin Mary looking at the Child Jesus, is steeped in a sense of ethereal grace. The art work in the faces, especially the foreheads, bears the hallmark of the Florentine School.

Nevers. The capital of the Nivernais area crossed by the R. Loire is famous for its earthenware pottery. Introduced into the locality c. 1565 by artists of Italian origin, it had one of the largest outputs in France during the reigns of Louis XIII and Louis XIV. The **Croux Gate**, a tall square tower with turrets and machicolations, was part of the town walls built in 1393.

Vichy, whose mineral springs were known in the days of Ancient Rome, was given spacious pump rooms by Napoleon III. The spa resort has a casino, theatres, concert halls, and sports amenities, offering visitors and those who come to "take the waters" a variety of entertainments throughout the summer season.

Right: **Tournus**. The old Gallic town that was once the home of the Edueni tribe, on the right bank of the R. Saône, became one of the largest monastic centres in France during the Merovingian Era (5th - 8th Centuries) when churches were built over St. Valerian's tomb.

In the 9th Century, monks who had been forced to flee the abbey on Noirmoutier as a result of the Viking invasions, brought St. Philibert's relics to Tournus. The abbey crypt, built at the end of the 10th Century, is outstanding for its height (11 ft. up to the vaulting). The roof of the crypt is supported by slender columns that have capitals decorated with foliage in the style of Ancient Greece and Rome.

Top, right: The **church in Paray-le-Monial**, which was made a basilica in 1875, is a fine example of Cluniac architecture. Built on the orders of St. Hugh, Abbot of Cluny (*p. 74*) from 1090 to 1109, it is striking for the simplicity of the West Front. It includes two square towers above the narthex.

Opposite, top: The **Puy-de-Dôme** is the highest (alt. 4,761 ft) and oldest volcano in the Puys range to the west of Clermont-Ferrand. It consists of a cone of waste formed by matter in fusion thrown up from the crater.

Opposite, bottom: **The church in Saint-Nectaire**, built c. 1160 in volcanic rock in a rugged but rustic setting, is a fine example of the Romanesque style as it developed in Auvergne. The chevet is elegantly designed. It compensates for the thrust from the octagonal belfry and is an attractive means of balancing the various volumes.

Right: **The church in Orcival**, founded in the early years of the 12th Century by monks from La Chaise-Dieu (*p. 82*), houses a wonderful statue of **the Virgin Mary in Majesty**. Venerated by pilgrims, the statue has retained its gold and silver decoration. Note the barrel vaulting in the nave and the ribbed vaulting in the side aisles.

Bottom: The **capitals** in the church in **Mozac** near Clermont-Ferrand are some of the oldest existing examples of Romanesque carvings in Auvergne. Their main feature is the use of very small figures. The **Resurrection Capital** shows the Holy Women at the tomb, holding jars of perfume. The strange gravity of their expressions and the nobility of their attitudes emphasised by the draping of their clothes is an example of the very best of sculpture as an art form.

The Cantal. The vast volcano in Cantal was worn away by glaciation and is now a succession of forests and lush pastures where cattle provide the milk that is used in the production of famous cheeses such as Fourme de Buron, Gaperon, and Cantal. The unspoiled environment and pure air are much appreciated by people who enjoy walking.

Opposite: **Brioude**. St. Julian's Basilica was built in the 11th and 12th Centuries on the spot where, according to tradition, a Roman centurion was martyred in 304 A.D. For many years, pilgrims came in large numbers to pray at St. Julian's tomb.

The basilica is almost 244 ft. in length, making it the largest Romanesque building in Auvergne. The warm colours come from the red sandstone and fine multi-coloured paving in the nave where the first few bays, the oldest in the building, are supported by massive pillars with engaged columns.

Top: **Clermont-Ferrand**. The interior of **the Basilica of Our Lady of the Port** (*Notre-Dame-du-Port*) built c. 1150 is an explicit expression of the austerity and solidity that are two of the main features of Romanesque buildings in Auvergne. In the transept (*left*), huge arches dating from the earlier, Carolingian building support the dome above squinches. The capitals on the columns in the chancel are eye-catching because of their expressiveness. One of them (*right*) depicts knights taking part in the First Crusade.

Bottom: **La Chaise-Dieu**. In 1150, Robert of Turland, former Canon of Brioude, founded a monastery whose influence was to spread to Italy and Spain. The splendid **tapestries** (*left*) hung above the closure in the chancel were made in Arras and Brussels in the early 16th Century. They illustrate the Old and New Testaments. The **Danse macabre** (*right*), a popular subject in the late 15th Century, shows the great and grand of this world (a rich man, a bishop, and a lady) next to the dead whom they will join one day.

Le Puy, the main town in the Vélay area, lies in an unusual setting consisting of a vast dip bristling with spurs of volcanic rock. Among them is **St. Michael's Rock** (*right*, 266 ft.) topped by a Romanesque chapel in the Byzantine style built at the end of the 11th Century on the site of a temple dedicated to Mercury.

Notre-Dame Cathedral, which is built on an outcrop of basalt, has a delightful set of **cloisters** (*bottom*) in which the multi-coloured mosaic decoration is a reminder of the Byzantine influence brought back from the Crusades. On one of the figurative capitals is a Centaur.

Top: The **Cévennes Hilltop Route** (*Corniche des Cévennes*) winds its way across mountainsides gashed by deep ravines as they slope down towards the Mediterranean coast. These vast stretches of woodland lie in the shadow of Mont Aigoual (alt. 5,093 ft.) (*left on the photo*).

Opposite, top: The **Eyrieux Hilltop Route** (*Corniche de l'Eyrieux*) crosses the rugged landscape of the **Vivarois Plateau**. From the ruins of **Pierre-Gourde Castle** is a panoramic view across the Eyrieux Valley dominated by woods on the slopes known as "*serres*", in fact sheer-sided peaks that are volcanic in origin.

Opposite, bottom: The **Navacelles Corrie** surrounded on all sides by tall limestone cliffs is the most spectacular beauty spot in the Causses. The river gouged out a meander then cut across it, after changing its original course.

Right: The **Demoiselles Cave** on Thaurac Plateau is said to be a marine cave dating from the Secondary Era. The walls were calcified at a later stage by the water running down the rock. This vast underground "cathedral" has a wide variety of stalagmites and stalactites, including this gigantic "Organ Loft".

The towers and octagonal belfry of the **Church of St. Faith's in Conques** (mid 11th - 12th Centuries) can be seen in the superb setting of the Ouche Gorge. In the Middle Ages, the abbey was a popular stopping-place on the road to Santiago de Compostela. The Conques treasure trove includes the striking **statue-reliquary of St. Faith** (10th Century) (*bottom*) covered in gold and precious stones.

Opposite: On the southern edge of the Massif Central are the **Grands Causses**, seemingly endless stretches of rough limestone terrain with a hard climate that provides very little grass for the flocks of sheep (*top: the **Méjean Causse***). Underground rivers have formed cavities in the rock, the most spectacular of all being the **Aven Armand** (*left.*), bristling with enormous stalagmites that constitute a veritable petrified forest.

The **Tarn Gorge** (*right*) is a deep sheer-sided valley in the Grands Causses. The river has made use of a number of natural crevices to cut its way across the limestone plateau.

On previous pages: The **Ardèche Gorge** cuts deeply into the Lower Vivaris Plateau. The **Madeleine Corrie** is one of the most impressive beauty spots in the 18-mile long river valley which can be visited by canoe.

Right: **Rodez**. The former capital of the Rouergue area grew up on a spot high above the R. Aveyron, between the hills drained by the R. Ségala and topped by the arid plateau known as the Causses. **Notre-Dame Cathedral** has a splendid Flamboyant Gothic belfry built in the early years of the 16th Century over an older tower. The top storeys are a succession of wide bays, statues of the Apostles, arcading, Flamboyant Gothic pinnacles, a terrace and balustrade.

Bottom: **Espalion** is a quiet little town attractively situated on the banks of the R. Lot which is spanned by the Old Bridge. The Renaissance-style Old Palace was once the residence of the town's governors.

The **Merle Towers** were part of an old fortress built in the 13th Century on a spur of rock on the borders of the Limousin and Auvergne. Considered for many years as totally impregnable, the castle was unable to withstand artillery fire and cannons placed on the surrounding hilltops could easily shower it with shot.

St. Stephen's Church (*église Saint-Etienne*) in **Lubersac**, a small village on the edge of Limousin's pastoral area, has a very rich set of 11th and 12th-century capitals. Stylistically, they are reminiscent of the ones in Moissac (*p. 107*). The **Annunciation Capital** shows Mary sitting on a spindle-backed chair, her hands open ready to receive the message brought to her by the Archangel, Gabriel, whose wings are spread wide. Note the headdress worn by Mary.

Top: The **Millevaches Plateau** (its name means "one thousand springs") provides the Limousin with its water supply. Countless rivers and springs rise on the plateau including the Creuse, Vézère, Vienne and Corrèze. The granite hills are desolate moorland covered with heather and fern, interspersed with a few stretches of forest.

Left: The old **Abbey of Le Moutier-d'Ahun** near Guéret was founded in the late 10th Century and was subject to the Rule of St. Benedict. The church houses a surprising set of **woodpanelling and choirstalls** carved between 1673 and 1683 by Simon Baüer, an artist from Auvergne. His work shows that he had perfect mastery of the techniques needed and that he had extensive knowledge of the vocabulary and forms of the Baroque era. The apse and chancel are decorated with a dazzling display of angels, enigmatic figures and animals from a fantasy world.

Opposite, bottom left: The **Collegiate Church of St. Peter** (*collégiale Saint-Pierre*) in **Le Dorat** dates from the 12th Century. It has an admirable multifoil doorway with festooned coving that is indicative of the Mozarabic influence, probably resulting from the arrival here of pilgrims from Santiago de Compostela.

Right: **Coussac-Bonneval Castle** (mid 14th Century) to the south of Limoges is the cradle of the illustrious Bonneval family whose most famous son was Claude-Alexandre, born in 1675. He began as a sailor before becoming an officer in an infantry regiment, taking part in the Italian Campaigns from 1701 to 1706 before entering the service of the Emperor of Austria. He then became a minister to Sultan Mahmud I and was given the title of "Humbaraci Ahmed Pasa". He organised the armies of the Ottoman Empire and spent the end of his life peacefully in Constantinople.

Bottom : **Limoges** is known worldwide for its porcelain. The town, which lies near seams of lead silicate and oxydes of other rare metals had been producing enamelwork since the 12th Century when Turgot, Intendant General of the Limousin, set up a porcelain works there in 1771. The works specialised in tableware and ornaments. The **Adrien-Dubouché Museum** contains more than 10,000 exhibits from works all over the world. The photograph shows a close-up of a centrepiece by the Pouyat works, made in 1878.

Bottom: **Poitiers** has several very interesting religious buildings, including the Church of Our Lady the Great (*Notre-Dame-la-Grande*) built in the Poitou Romanesque style. The **Church of St. Hilary the Great**, built in 1049, used to have a timber ceiling before it was burnt down in the early years of the 12th Century. In order to support the weight of the new stone roof, the architect divided each of the side aisles in half and placed columns in the nave linked to the side walls and topped with domes and pendentives.

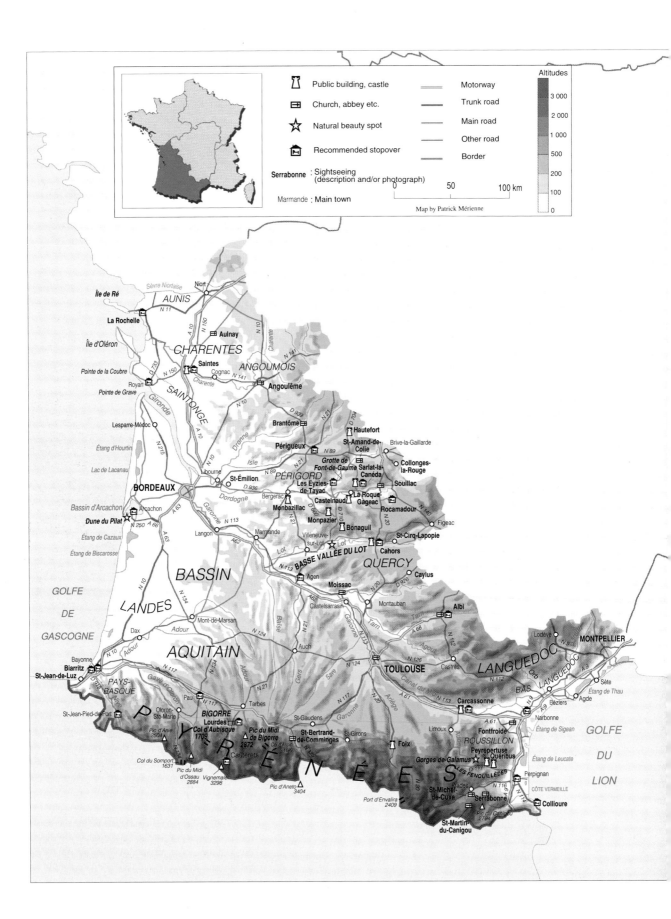

SOUTH-WESTERN FRANCE

Charentes. Périgord. Quercy. Aquitaine Basin. Pyrenees. Roussillon. Languedoc.

The Aubisque Pass in the **Pyrenees**.

Rocamadour in Quercy.

The **Charentes** region includes the old provinces of Saintonges (around Saintes), **Angoumois** (centred on Angoulême), and **Aunis** (around La Rochelle), transitional rural areas lying between the Massif Central and the Atlantic coast. **Périgord** and **Quercy** have alternating plateaux which are only sparsely populated, and valleys in which most of the economic life is concentrated. This is a mainly agricultural region, famous for its preserved duck and goose, its foie gras, and its truffles, mushrooms that grow under the earth around oaks and hazelnut trees.

The **Aquitaine Basin** is a lush farming area with particularly fertile soil (sediment and alluvial plains) and a generous climate. Fruit trees and, more especially, vines are an integral part of the landscape here. To the west is the huge forest of the **Landes**, planted in the mid 19th Century in order to improve the badly-drained plain and sandy subsoil. It covers a triangle with an area of 14,000 sq. km and has millions of maritime pines.

Stretching from the Atlantic to the Mediterranean, the **Pyrenees** have well-sheltered valleys where the population is fairly dense and powerful mountains with sheer slopes topped by glaciers. At the eastern end, the range plunges down into the sea in the **Roussillon**, an area more open to a Mediterranean way of life. The **Lower Languedoc**, a crescent extending over a distance of some 25 miles along the shores of the Gulf of Lions leads into Provence. It is a sandy plain dotted with inland lakes and covered with vineyards.

Top: **La Rochelle** was a Protestant stronghold when the Wars of Religion laid waste to the country between 1562 and 1598. It was not until 1628 that Cardinal Richelieu overcame the resistance put up by the local people, who were starving after a prolonged blockade. The mouth of the harbour created during the reign of Eleanor of Aquitaine was defended by the St. Nicholas Tower and the Chain Tower, both of them built in the 14th Century. The geographical situation of La Rochelle midway along the coast between Nantes and Bordeaux enabled shipowners to develop trade with Canada, Louisiana and the West Indies in the 18th Century. Nowadays, it is trawlers and yachts, for which the new Port des Minimes was built, that bring life to the seafront.

Left: **The Island of Ré** which stretches over a distance of some 19 miles offshore from La Rochelle is now linked to *terra firma* by a huge bridge. The locals take advantage of an exceptionally mild climate to produce wonderful early spring vegetables and an outstanding wine that has the tang of seaweed in it. The long beaches lined with pinewoods are a delight for holidaymakers in search of fresh, clean air. Near Saint-Martin-de-Ré are the ruins of the **old Cistercian Abbey of Les Châteliers** founded in the 12th Century.

Aulnay: St. Peter's Church (*église Saint-Pierre*), built from 1140 to 1170 on the road to Santiago de Compostela, has admirable carvings that are a masterpiece of Romanesque architecture as it developed in the Saintonge area. On the South door, the second and third lines of coving bear carvings of the prophets, the Apostles, and the Elders of the Apocalypse. The first and fourth lines of coving are decorated with lively carvings of fantastic figures and animals.

It was in **Saintes**, the capital of the Santones during the Roman Occupation, that the Latin poet, Ausonius (c. 310 - c. 395 A.D.), died. It was he who wrote so lyrically about the scenery in southern Gaul. The **Germanicus Arch** built in the year 19 A.D, marked the end of the Roman roads from Poitiers and Limoges. Note the grooved pilasters topped by Corinthian capitals at the corners of the pillars.

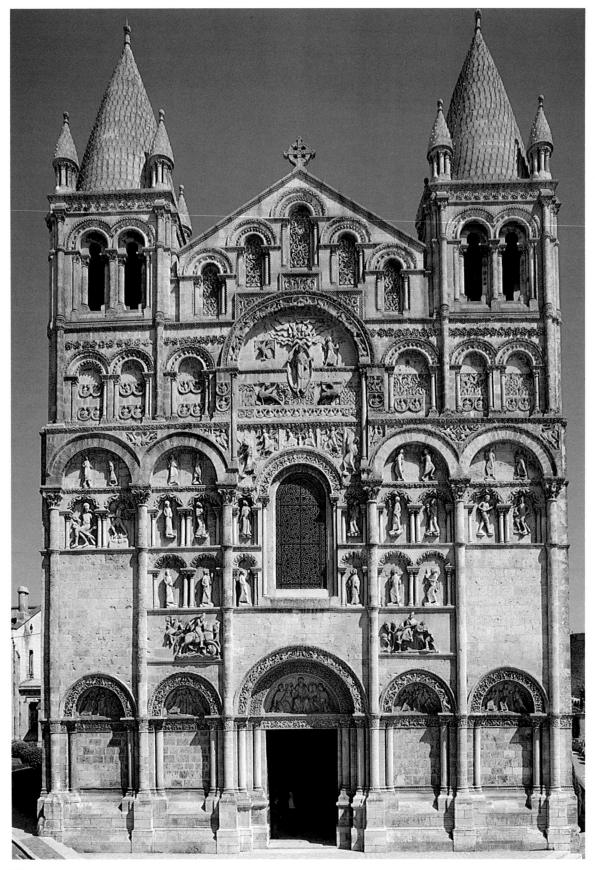

Angoulême: St. Peter's Cathedral (*cathédrale Saint-Pierre*, 12th Century) has a very ornate West Front carved in the Poitou style and is outstanding for its superimposed registers of arches. The Last Judgement is depicted with 70 figures standing around Christ in Majesty. Above the first door, to the right, is a battle scene inspired by the *Song of Roland*. The carvings are effective and full of movement, thanks to the decorative friezes of foliage, medallions and all sorts of animals.

Right: **Périgueux** was, for many years, divided between the walled town that had grown up out of the ancient Vesuna and the powerful monastic community of Puy-Saint-Front which attracted crowds of pilgrims who came to pray on the tomb of the preacher who had converted Périgord to Christianity. A municipal charter drawn up in 1251 put an end to two centuries of conflict. **St. Front's Cathedral** is the most outstanding example of the domed churches of Périgord. Completed in 1173 to a design reminiscent of the Church of the Disciples in Constantinople, it is laid out in the form of a Greek Cross. The bell turrets were added during later restoration.

The north wall of the **Château Barrière** has a Flamboyant Gothic entrance.

Opposite, bottom left: **Brantôme** on the banks of the R. Dronne is one of the most attractive of all the beauty spots in Périgord. To the right are the 11th-century Romanesque belltower and the buildings constructed in the 18th Century on the site of an abbey originally founded in 769 A.D. by Charlemagne. The famous chronicler **Pierre de Bourdeilles**, better-known under his pen-name, Brantôme, the commendary Abbot at the end of the 16th Century, took pleasure giving a complacent account of the private life of the Grand and Famous of the day, in his *Memoirs..*

Bottom: On the borders of the Limousin and White Périgord stands the **Château de Hautefort** in the middle of a superb formal park on a hillside overlooking the village. Built between 1625 and 1670 in the Classical style, with the exception of the domes which came from the earlier building, it was the home of Marie de Hautefort, lady-in-waiting to Anne of Austria. Marie had a platonic love affair with Louis XIII.

Sarlat-la-Canéda, capital of Dark Périgord, was a prosperous town for many years and it has retained the fine patrician houses built for its rich merchants, its upper middle classes, and its magistrates from the 13th Century onwards. There is still a bustling market here, with local produce such as foie gras, truffles and walnuts for sale. The **La Boétie Residence**, built in the Renaissance style, was the birthplace of Etienne de La Boétie (1530-1565), loyal friend of Montaigne who stated the case against tyranny in his work entitled *Discourse on Voluntary Servitude*.

La Roque-Gageac is said to be the most beautiful spot in the Dordogne Valley. The houses, roofed with stone slabs and tiles, huddle close to each other at the foot of the tall cliff. Some of them even cling on to the lower slopes.

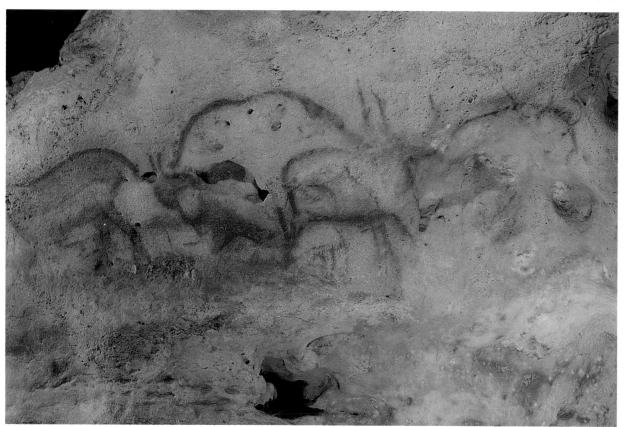

The **Font-de-Gaume Cave** contains a set of prehistoric cave paintings that are of outstanding interest. The drawings of reindeer, bison and mammoths show the mastery of the craftsmen and are thought, by specialists, to date from the Magdalanian Era (10,000 - 15,000 years ago). Not far away is the National Prehistory Museum (*musée national de la préhistoire*) in Les Eyzies-de-Tayac (*p. 5*) where you can see collections of artefacts and works of art that are important as an illustration of the development of the cavedweller civilisation.

Set back from the Vézère Valley is the amazing fortified church in **Saint-Amand-de-Coly**. Its powerful porch-belfry built of fine, golden limestone, afforded protection for the Augustinian abbey in the 12th Century. Near roof level were corbels supporting lookout turrets.

The **hilltop town of Monpazier**, founded by King Edward I of England, Duke of Aquitaine, was part of a system of defence that was set up in Périgord from 1267 onwards. The admirably well-preserved central square is flanked by houses built over arcades.

The town is a quadrilateral one-quarter of a mile mile in length and 238 yds. wide. It was originally defended by six fortified gates, of which three have survived. The streets cut across each other at right angles.

Left : **Collonges-la-Rouge** is a strange town of mansions built of purple schist and flanked by turrets in a delightful country setting. In the 16th Century, Collonges was the favourite place of residence for the great officials in the Viscounty of Turenne which included more than 1,000 villages in the Sarlat area, Upper Quercy and Limousin.

Opposite, top : The church in **Saint-Cirq-Lapopie** seems to be standing guard on a terrace more than 260 ft. above the R. Lot. The spot, named after the martyrdom of St. Cyr during the reign of Diocletian, has been highly-prized since Gallo-Roman times. Richard the Lionheart tried

to capture it in 1198, followed by fellow Englishmen during the One Hundred Years' War. It was Henry of Navarre, the future King Henri IV, who demolished the castle in 1580.

The village has numerous fine corbelled houses with Gothic or Renaissance windows. They stand at the foot of the massive belltower on the church built in the 15th Century.

Right : The interior of the West Front in the old **minster in Souillac** (late 12th Century) at the confluence of the rivers Corrèze and Dordogne was decorated with the remains of the old doorway damaged by the Huguenots in 1573. The bas-relief representing **the prophet Isaiah**, which bears a marked resemblance to the carving of Jeremiah on the pier in Moissac (*p. 107*), has a superb feeling of movement resembling a dance step.

On previous pages: The castles of **Castelnaud** on the left bank of the Dordogne and **Beynac** on the opposite bank were locked in endless conflict throughout the Middle Ages. During the One Hundred Years' War, Castelnaud was captured several times by both the French and the English.

Right: **Cahors** owed its prosperity in the 13th Century to trade and banking. Lombard financiers established in the town of Cahors made it Europe's leading financial centre. The town was handed over to the English by the King of France in 1360 and was ruined by the end of the One Hundred Years' War.

The **Valentré Bridge**, built on the orders of the town's merchants between 1308 and 1378, was designed as a veritable fortress standing guard over the river. The central tower provided an excellent lookout post keeping watch over the surrounding area while the other two towers, which have no portcullis, protected the bridge itself.

Bottom: **Bonaguil**, a fortress on the borders of Dark Périgord and Quercy is a fine example of defensive architecture. Built in the 15th and 16th Centuries, it was one of the first strongholds to integrate the use of firearms in its system of defence.

Moissac. The Benedictine abbey founded in the 7th Century by a monk from St. Wandrille's Abbey in Normandy reached the height of its power and influence in the 11th and 12th Centuries. It was then that the cloisters were built, with slender marble columns topped by widely differing capitals, and that the South Portal was added. Its tympanum is supported by a **jamb** that is famous throughout the world of Romanesque architecture. The single block of stone is decorated with lions standing on their hind legs; their purpose is to guard the entrance to the church. On the sides are effigies of St. Paul and **St. Jeremiah** which, from the artistic point of view, are among the most outstanding masterpieces in Moissac. Backing onto the column but detached from it, they are forerunners of the statue-columns of the Late Romanesque Period which are particularly common in the Paris Basin (*p. 14*).

The **Lower Lot Valley** has cut out a course for itself through the arid plateaux of Quercy. The river flows between hard limestone scarp slopes topped with superb chestnut groves. Farming is carried out within the meanders. Quercy is best-known for the Cahors wines that have been popular since the Middle Ages and for tobacco (the first plants were imported from America in the 16th Century).

The **vineyards of the Bordeaux area** cover more than 130,000 hectares to each side of the Garonne and Dordogne Valleys and along the left bank of the Gironde Estuary downstream from Bordeaux. Approximately 8,000 "châteaux" produce wines whose names are sufficient measure of their reputation. Saint-Estèphe, Mouton-Rothschild, Margaux, Pauillac, Lafite etc. in the **Upper Médoc** produce a red wine that ages remarkably well. The vineyards in **Sauternes** and **Barsac** are famous for their sweet white wines obtained from grapes harvested when they have reached a very advanced stage of ripeness. **Château-Yquem** is the most famous of all. **L'Entre-Deux-Mers** (*opposite, top left: the grape harvest at Château Clavier*) is the land of fruity, dry whites. On the right bank of the R. Dordogne, clinging onto the limestone hillsides, is **Saint-Emilion**, one of the oldest wine-growing areas in the region (the Gallo-Roman poet Ausonius (*p. 97*) had a villa in the midst of vineyards there). It produces red wines with a wonderful bouquet (*bottom: the grape harvest at Château Bellevue in Montagne*). Further north is the generous **Pomerol** area whose wines are warm to the palate, with a deep robe and a subtle bouquet with just a hint of truffle.

Top: **Monbazillac** (mid 16th Century) is a pleasing combination of military and Renaissance architecture. Huge round towers, a parapet walkway and machicolations topped by elegant dormer windows flank the façade with its transomed windows. The vineyards, growing mainly Sauvignon grapes, produce a smooth white wine with a golden colour.

Bordeaux grew up along the left bank of a wide bend in the R. Garonne. In 56 B.C, the Roman army invaded the small town that was the home of the Celtic Bituriges tribe. The Romans then set about organising trade and launching the planting of grapes, thereby creating the two sectors that have been giving Bordeaux its prosperity ever since.

The old town of Bordeaux is an outstanding example of 18th-century urban planning. The **Place de la Bourse** (*bottom*) designed by the Gabriels (father and son) and the **Place du Parlement** (*middle left*) bear witness to the town's wealth in the days when it was the country's leading port.

Opposite, top: The **Pilat Dune** is more than one mile long and rises to a height of 370 ft. above the Atlantic Ocean. Formed by the wind and maritime currents, it is slowly but surely submerging the forests in the Landes.

Opposite, bottom: **Biarritz**. This old fishing village on the Basque coast was turned upside down in the mid 19th Century when it became a cosmopolitan seaside resort attracting Russian, British and Spanish aristocrats, royalty, artists and writers. During the "Roaring Twenties", the town acquired luxurious holiday villas and sumptuous parties were the order of the day. Chaplin, Picasso, and Sarah Bernhardt were the leading lights in Biarritz' high society. The remains of this past now combine with more recent constructions to give the resort its own, very special charm.

In the background is the **Rhune** (alt. 2,925 ft.), from whose summit there is a wonderful panoramic view of the ocean and the Basque Country.

Top: Once a whaling harbour, **Saint-Jean-de-Luz** now specialises in sardine, tunny and anchovy fishing. It is also an elegant seaside resort with a huge beach.

Overleaf: The **Pyrenees** stretch from the Atlantic to the Mediterranean, a distance of more than 300 miles, forming a gigantic barrier between France and Spain. The range came into being sixty million years ago when the European insular shelf collided with the Iberian Peninsula, causing geological upheaval. The central area is dotted with granite forming mountains like the Néouvielle Range (*to the right of the photograph, taken from the Aspin Pass*), all of them worn away by glacial erosion.

Top: **The Basque Country** consists of a wild landscape exposed to the rainfall that sweeps in from the Atlantic. The population is strongly attached to its traditions and many people are still employed in sheep-rearing and related activities. The locals are descended from the Basques who came originally from the Ebre Valley in Spain. Their language (*euskara*) mysteriously escaped the Indo-European influence.

Bottom: **Lourdes**. On 11th February 1858, Bernadette Soubirous stated categorically that the Virgin Mary had appeared before her near the Massabielle Rock. Nowadays, the small town situated at the foot of the Bigorre Mountain has become the most popular place of pilgrimage in the world, attracting almost five million visitors every year.

Opposite, top: The **Pic du Midi de Bigorre** stands out high above the Central Pyrenees Range, at an altitude of 9,311 ft. The summit can be reached by cable car. On it is an observatory and a scientific research institute specialising mainly in the solar crown, lunar cartography and cosmic radiation.

Opposite, bottom: Between the Garonne Plain and the high mountains in the centre of the Pyrenees are the foothills of the range clearly bearing the mark of man's intervention. From the **Pic du Jer** near Lourdes, the view extends over this part of **Bigorre** and it is easy to pick out the different types of farming, with fields under cultivation and meadows.

Top: **Toulouse** owes its nickname of "The Pink City" to the use of brick, the most common material in its public buildings. The **Dominicans' Church,** the first monastery founded for the Order of the Friars Preacher by St. Dominic in 1215, has a vast nave with two bays. The ribbed vaulting is beautifully laid out. Twenty-two ribs radiate out from the pillar in the chancel known as the "palm tree". The lightness of brick and its ability to adhere to mortar enabled the architect to build this vaulted roof, which is unusually large, as far back as 1292. It is a forerunner of the fan vaulting that became popular at the end of the Gothic period.

Bottom: The old castle of the Counts of **Foix** in the heart of Ariège still has its watch towers and system of defence. In the background are the snow-covered peaks of the central part of the Pyrenees Range.

Opposite: In the 13th Century, **Albi** provided a refuge for followers of the Cathar doctrine who were being pursued by the armies of the Inquisition. **St. Cecilia's Cathedral**, built from 1282 onwards to celebrate the victory of the Roman Catholic Church, looks rather like a fortress. The chancel has a superb collection of choirstalls topped by a frieze of cherubs.

Top: **Peyrepertuse**, perched on a spur of rock, is the largest of the Cathar castles. Mentioned in documents dating back to the 9th Century, it became the property of the Counts of Barcelona in 1111, then fell into the hands of the King of Aragon before being sold to the King of France in 1226. It was used as a refuge by the Cathari and was captured after three days of fighting in November 1240. St. Louis made it the main fortress overlooking the Roussillon.

Bottom: **Quéribus** near Peyrepertuse was the last bastion of the Cathari. It did not fall until 1256, and then only as a result of treachery. Built on a narrow outcrop of rock, its huge keep stands high above the Roussillon Plain. In the distance is the Canigou mountain covered in snow.

Opposite, top: **Les Fenouillèdes** is a wild area of medium-sized mountains between the Corbières and Roussillon regions. Its slopes are covered with scrub and green oaks that have been cleared in some places to leave space for vineyards. It enjoys an exceptionally high number of hours of sunshine and produces Maury, a much-appreciated sweet wine.

Opposite, bottom: The Benedictine Abbey of **Saint-Martin-du-Canigou** perches on the mountainside at an altitude of 3,555 ft. All that remains of the original buildings erected in the 11th Century are three galleries in the cloisters (the fourth gallery, overlooking the mountain, has been restored) and the church topped with a massive belfry that looks more like a castle keep.

On previous pages and top: Situated in a narrow ridge separating the Massif Central from the Pyrenees, **Carcassonne** stands guard over the corridor between the Mediterranean and the Atlantic and between France and Spain. The Romans built the first castle here, and it was reinforced by the Visigoths in the 5th Century. In 1130, the Lords of Trencavel, Viscounts of Carcassonne, commissioned the building of the **Count's Castle** (*top*), a gem of mediaeval military architecture. The fortress was annexed to France after the Albigensian Crusade (1224-1226). Louis IX and, later, Philip the Bold built a second outer wall, making the stronghold virtually impregnable.

Right: The Romanesque priory in **Serrabonne** clings onto the eastern slopes of the Canigou Range. In its austere church dating from the 11th - 12th Centuries, there is a very ornate pink marble gallery. The columns are decorated with capitals and have delicately carved archivolts. Carvings of lions (in homage to Christ, the "Lion of Judah"?) can be seen all over the building among other mythological beasts, angels and a profusion of plants.

Top: The **Galamus Gorge** was carved out of the final outcrop of limestone rock in the Corbières area by the R. Agly. From the road, there are a number of spectacular views over this 1,625 ft. deep chasm.

Bottom, left: The cathedral in **Saint-Bertrand-de-Comminges** in the Upper Garonne Valley was built in 1073 on the orders of Bishop Bertrand on the site of Lugdunum Convenarum, which had been founded in 72 B.C. by Pompey the Great. The cloisters, built between the 12th and 15th Centuries, are famous for the Evangelists Pillar. Matthew, Mark, Luke and John are carved in antique style in a column used originally in the Roman town.

Bottom, right: Founded in 883 A.D. in the depths of the Leitera Valley, the Abbey of **Saint-Michel-de-Cuxa** reached the height of its influence and power in the 11th Century under the leadership of Abbot Oliva. Sold off in 1793, the buildings were dismantled and the stone dispersed. In 1913, the American sculptor G.G. Bernard found some of it and took it to the Metropolitan Museum of New York. Two of the cloister galleries were rebuilt there. The carnal realism of the carvings on the capitals shows the power of mediaeval mysticism.

Opposite: **Fontfroide Abbey** nestles in the depths of a valley in the Corbières area filled with cypress trees and arbutus. In 1093, a few monks in search of a place of prayer founded the monastery that became a daughter-house of Cîteaux in 1143. In the Middle Ages, Fontfroide remained a centre of orthodox doctrine in the face of Catharism. The elegant galleries in the **cloisters** (*top*) with their ribbed vaulting date from the 13th Century. The **chapter house** (*bottom*) has quadripartite Romanesque vaulting supported on very slender marble colonettes.

Top: **Collioure** is a small port situated in a superb setting at the foot of the **Albères Hills** where the slopes are covered with the vineyards that produce Banyuls. The flower-decked houses huddling up against the royal castle and church, the terraces, the brightly-coloured boats and the nets spread out to dry have inspired countless artists, among them Derain, Braque and Matisse. Later, it was Foujita and Picasso who captured the spot for all time on their canvases. Collioure is famous for its anchovies, which are caught at night by "lamplight".

Bottom: **Montpellier**, the historical capital of **Lower Languedoc**, gets its name from the spice trade that was prevalent from the 10th Century onwards on "Spicers' Hill" (*Mont des Epiciers*) or Monspistillarius. Doctors interested in the therapeutic virtues of spices set up a medical faculty here in the 12th Century, and this marked the beginnings of the town's university tradition. Montpellier's many fine buildings were erected for the rich upper middle classes. It was they who, in the late 17th Century, commissioned the Promenade du Peyrou opening onto a triumphant arch in honour of Louis XIV and the many luxurious mansions in the old town.

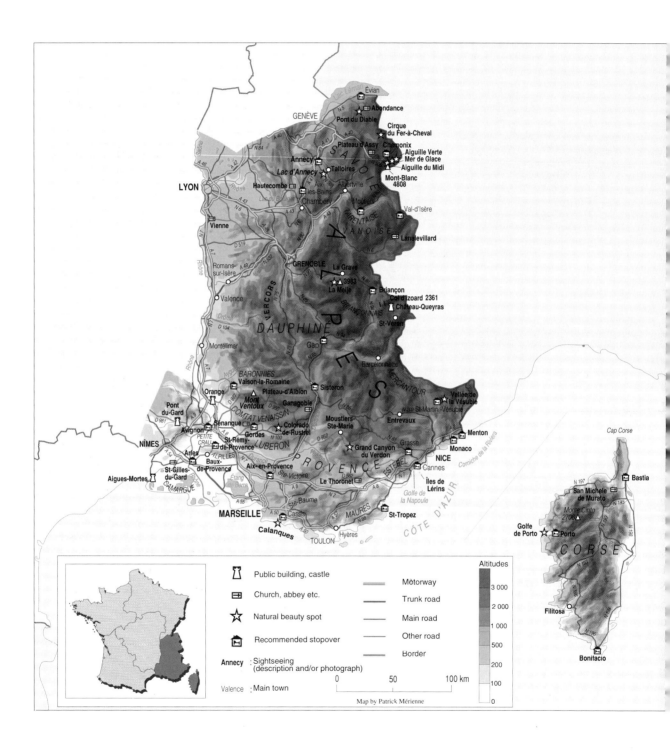

Évian
GENÈVE
★ ◨ Abondance
N 5
★ Pont du Diable
Cirque
du Fer-à-Cheval
Plateau d'Assy
Chamonix
SAVOIE
Aiguille Verte
★★★ Mer de Glace
Annecy ◨ ★ Aiguille du Midi
Lac d'Annecy ★ Talloires
LYON
Hautecombe ◨⊞ Albertville
Aix-
les-Bains
Chambéry
Moûtiers
Val-d'Isère
TARENTAISE
Vienne ◨
VANOISE
Lanslevillard
ALPES
La Grave
GRENOBLE ○ ★ 3983
La Meije
Romans-
sur-Isère
Briançon ◨
Col d'Izoard 2361
BRIANÇONNAIS
St-Véran
Château-Queyras ⛫
Valence ○
DAUPHINÉ
Gap ○
VERCORS
Barcelonnette ○
Montélimar ○
MERCANTOUR
BARONNIES
Vaison-la-Romaine ★
▲ Plateau-d'Albion
Sisteron ◨
Vallée de
la Vésubie ★
Orange ○ *Mont*
Ventoux ▲ Ganagobie ⊞
St-Martin -Vésubie
Pont
du-Gard
LUBERON ○ Sénanque ⊞ Gordes
COMTAT VENAISSIN
Colorado
de-Rustrel ★
Moustiers-
Ste-Marie
Entrevaux ○
Grasse ○
Menton ⊞
St-Rémy-
de-Provence ◨⊞
AVIGNON ◨
NÎMES
Grand Canyon
du Verdon ★
Monaco ◨
PETITE
CRAU
Arles ◨
LES
BAUX ○ Baux-
de-Provence
PROVENCE
NICE ◨
St-Gilles-
du-Gard ⊞
Aix-en-Provence
Cannes
Aigues-Mortes ⛫
Étang
de
Berre
Ste-Victoire
Le Thoronet ⊞
ESTEREL
Îles de
Lérins
CAMARGUE
Ste-Baume
MAURES
Golfe de
la Napoule
CÔTE D'AZUR
MARSEILLE
Cassis ◨
St-Tropez ◨
★ Calanques
TOULON
Hyères ○

Cap Corse

CORSE

Bastia ⊞
San Michele
de Murato ⊞
N 197
N 193
N 193
Monte Cinto
2706 ▲
Golfe
de Porto ★ ◨ Porto
Filitosa ○
N 193
Bonifacio ⊞

Altitudes

⛫	Public building, castle		Motorway
⊞	Church, abbey etc.		Trunk road
★	Natural beauty spot		Main road
◨	Recommended stopover		Other road
Annecy	: Sightseeing (description and/or photograph)		Border
Valence	: Main town		

3 000
2 000
1 000
500
200
100
0

0   50   100 km

Map by Patrick Mérienne

SOUTH-EASTERN FRANCE

Savoy. Dauphiné. Provence. The Riviera. Corsica.

L'Aiguille Verte (alt. 13,396 ft.) in the Mont-Blanc Range.

The village of **Les Baux-de-Provence**.

The **Northern Alps**, which cover the historical regions of **Savoy** and **Dauphiné**, form an area of majestic peaks and mighty glaciers. The mountains were created as a result of the Hercynian folding that broke the earth's crust some six hundred million years ago, during the Primary Era. The subsidence that then occurred during the Secondary Era (two hundred million years ago) led to the creation of a maritime trough which was slowly filled in by deposits of limestone and sand. During the Tertiary Era, which began sixty million years ago, a geological upheaval caused the layers to slip, forming the mountains in the Briançon area and the **Vanoise**. Later, a second upheaval, probably caused by the shifting of the continents, created the **Mont-Blanc, Ecrins,** and **Mercantour** in the **Southern Alps.** The bare mountainsides, wide luminous valleys and expanses of stony ground in these areas are the main characteristics of Southern French landscapes.

Provence, through which flow the lower reaches of the **R. Rhône**, is broken up by folded mountain ranges such as the **Baronnies, Ventoux, Lubéron, Alpilles, Sainte-Victoire and Sainte-Baume**. Between them are the plains, in which the soil was improved as far back as the Roman Era thanks to the introduction of irrigation; they are now covered in crops - fruit and vegetables in the **Comtat Venaissin** and **Petite Crau**, vines and olive trees at the foot of the Lubéron and Alpilles, and rice in **Camargue**.

The **Riviera**, where the mountains meet the sea and the sun, stretches from Toulon to **Menton** in a succession of dazzling landscapes consisting of creeks, uplands (**Maures and Esterel**), gulfs (**Saint-Tropez** and **Napoule**), the **Baie des Anges** and the **Riviera Hilltop Route** (*corniche de la Riviera*).

Corsica has the highest altitudes of all the islands in the Mediterranean, reaching a height of 8,794 ft. at **Monte Cinto**. Its 625 miles of rocky coastline are deeply gashed with alternating deep gulfs, tiny coves and sheer-sided headlands. Inland, the mountains and high valleys are dotted with picturesque hilltop villages.

Lyons. Magnificently situated at the confluence of the rivers Rhône and Saône at the foot of the Fourvière and Croix-Rousse Hills, Lyons has taken full advantage of its geographical position over the past twenty years. Having established links with Northern Europe while being connected to the Mediterranean Basin through the Rhône and lying at the crossroads of Europe, between France, Italy and Switzerland, the former capital of Gaul is both a prosperous commercial centre (with fairs and exhibitions), a busy industrial city (mechanical engineering, chemicals), a major university town and a leader in the medical field. The **Place Bellecour** centring on the equestrian statue of Louis XIV lies in the heart of the peninsula formed by the Rhône and Saône which is also the busiest part of the town. **Notre-Dame Basilica** standing on Fourvière Hill was built after the French defeat in the Franco-Prussian War of 1870-1871. It is a surprising combination of mediaeval and Byzantine architecture.

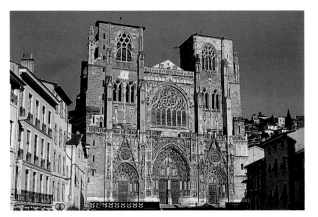

Vienne was a Roman colony fifty years before Julius Caesar conquered Gaul. The **Temple of Augustus and Livia** (*p.5*), built shortly before the Christian era, is a reminder of this period when public buildings and private houses earned the town the name of "Beautiful Vienne". **St. Maurice' Cathedral** (12th - 16th Centuries) combines Romanesque and Gothic features. The West Front has three Flamboyant Gothic doorways on which the coving bears a particularly refined, inventive type of carving.

Hautecombe Abbey was built on the west bank of the Lac du Bourget c. 1139. Fifty years later, it became the burial place of the House of Savoy. The last King of Italy, Umberto II, was laid to rest in Hautecombe in 1983. The church was restored in the 19th Century in the Gothic "troubadour" style in which the main feature is the over-exuberant decoration. In 1992, the Cistercian monks who had been living in the abbey since Savoy was annexed to France in 1860 left for the priory in Ganagobie (*p. 143*) in Haute-Provence.

The **Devil's Bridge Gorge** (*gorges du Pont du Diable*) was cut into the Chablais marble by the Dranse de Morzine. Because of the type of rock, the river has worn it very smooth and produced some very strange shapes (giants' stewpots). The footbridge from which people can visit the gorge runs along the rock face 195 ft. above the floor of the gorge. Deposits have coloured the rock in shades of yellow ochre, blue and green.

Top: The **Lac d'Annecy**, which is almost nine miles long, fills a valley formed by glacial erosion. Talloires, an elegant holiday resort on the right bank, stands opposite Duingt Castle.

Middle: **Annecy** stands in a delightful setting on the shores of the lake, flanked by mountains on all sides. In the 16th Century, the town replaced Geneva as the regional capital. The old town around the Isle Palace (12th Century) is filled with colourful house fronts on the banks of the R. Thiou.

Bottom: **Abondance**. The community founded in the 11th Century by Augustinian canons was made an abbey c. 1130. As owner of the entire valley, the abbey enjoyed enormous prosperity until the 15th Century and its influence extended throughout the Northern Alps and Franche-Comté. The **frescoes in the cloisters** are said to have been made between 1410 and 1420 by an artist who trained in the studio of the master painter from Piedmont, Giacomo Jacquerio. The scenes, illustrating the Life of the Virgin Mary, include details of everyday life in the Savoy of the 15th Century.

The **Horseshoe Corrie** (*cirque du Fer-à-Cheval*) bet-ween the Chablais area and the Mont-Blanc range is a vast semi-circle of mighty walls of rock carved out of the limestone of the Northern Pre-Alps. Numerous waterfalls cascade down the sides of the Tenneverge, in which the highest peak is the Come du Chamois (alt. 9,708 ft.) crea-ting a permanent background noise that is a characteristic feature of the spot.

The **Tarentaise** area in the upper Isère Valley has succeeded in preserving certain traditions which are brought back to life during folk festivals. In **Peisey-Nancroix**, the Mountain Festival held on 15th August brings out the young girls dressed in the beautiful tradi-tional costume including the local headdress. In the Tarentaise area, it is called the "*frontière*" because it forms three peaks that frame the forehead. Richly deco-rated with gold and silver braid, it dates back to the 16th Century. The young men dress as chimneysweeps, the trade that their grandfathers and great-grandfathers before them plied in the plain during the months when there was no farm work to be done.

Rising to an altitude of 15,626 ft, the **Mont-Blanc Range** is both the highest of the European mountains and the one with the greatest variety of contours. The summit (*top*) consists of a succession of snow-capped domes high above the **Bossons Glacier** over four miles long, the tip of which lies on the forest level near houses. Mont Blanc was first climbed on 8th August 1786 by Dr. Michel Paccard and Jacques Balmat.

The **Aiguille du Midi** (*opposite*) is a formidable up-sweep of rock above the Chamonix Valley. A breathtaking cable car ride takes visitors up to the summit at an altitude of 12,486 ft. The panoramic view from the terrace on the central peak is totally unobstructed. It extends across the French Alps including the Aiguille Verte (*p. 127*) and Grandes Jorasses, to the Alps in Switzerland and Italy.

The **Sea of Ice** (*Mer de Glace, bottom*) is almost nine miles long and is easily accessible by the Montenvers rack-and-pinion railway which was inaugurated in 1908. The glacier is 1,300 ft. thick and it advances by 292 ft. every year. It carries with it an impressive quantity of rocky debris that gives it a greyish appearance.

Top: At the confluence of the rivers Isère and Drac, in the centre of a corrie deep in the mountains, lies **Grenoble** which, despite long-lasting communications problems, has succeeded in becoming the economic and intellectual capital of the Alps. The 1968 Winter Olympics gave it extensive sports amenities. From the Bastille Fort cable car, it is easy to see the different stages in the town's development from the old town centred on the Place Grenette to the large modern housing estates on the outskirts.

Opposite: **La Grave** and **La Meije**. At the foot of the Meije range is La Grave, one of the foremost mountaineering resorts in Dauphiné, on the edge of the Ecrins Range.

The Grand Pic de la Meije (alt. 12,945 ft.) remained unconquered for many years. Seventeen expeditions tried to reach the summit before Mr. Boileau de Castelnau finally succeeded, on 16th August 1877, accompanied by mountain guides from Saint-Christophe-en-Oisans. The Ecrins Range, where the average altitude is the highest anywhere in the Alps, is particularly popular with hillwalkers and mountaineers.

Bottom **Lanslevieillard**, perched at an altitude of 4,875 ft in the Upper Maurienne Valley, has a chapel of modest proportions housing a set of frescoes in a perfect state of conservation. Painted in the 15th Century, they are interesting for the many different attitudes of the figures and the vast range of colours used.

Briançon, the highest town in Europe lying at an altitude of 4,293 ft, occupies a strategic position at the junction of the two roads leading into Italy. Vauban was ordered by Louis XIV to make Briançon impregnable after the town had been set on fire by the Duke of Savoy in 1692. In just one week, the engineer had drawn up the plans for the fortifications in the **upper town** (*bottom right on the photograph*) which included a bastioned wall protected by a ring of small forts distributed across the neighbouring hilltops. In 1815, after the defeat at Waterloo, an Austro-Sardinian army was unable to capture the citadel, despite a siege lasting four months.

The **Collegiate Church of Our Lady** (*top*) built during the first half of the 18th Century stands high above the upper town. Each of its towers bears a sun dial. Painted in 1719 in the Baroque style, the one on the left is particularly elegant. In the background are the eastern slopes of the Ecrins Range (*p. 134*).

Top: The **Izoard Pass** at an altitude of 7,670 ft, links the Briançon area to the Queyras. Beyond the wooded valleys, the road rises in a series of hairpin bends up through a landscape that becomes increasingly bare until it reaches the **Casse Déserte**. This austere spot, a slope full of gullies bristling with jagged rocks, shows the destructive results of the considerable daily variations in temperature. The dilatation of the rock during the day and its contraction at night cause the rock to disintegrate, leading to a levelling of the landscape.

Opposite, top: **Saint-Véran** in the Queyras is the highest village in Europe. Lying at an altitude of more than 6,500 ft, its chalets are built on an open, south-facing terrace.

Opposite, bottom: **Château-Queyras** is built on a glacial strait guarding the entrance to the Guil Valley. The earlier fortifications were reinforced by Vauban in the latter years of the 17th Century.

The **Vercors** in Dauphiné is the large range of hills forming the Northern Pre-Alps. It consists of folds piled up under the effect of the lifting of the axial area of the Alps during the Tertiary Era (*p. 127*). The high limestone plateau covered with beech and conifer forests has been gashed by rivers and worn away beneath the ground by the passage of underground streams. Although this was traditionally a stock-breeding area, it has become a popular tourist venue, especially with potholers and cross-country skiers. The Upper Cholet Valley, also known as **Combe Laval**, is dwarfed by an awesome wall of limestone rock more than 1,950 ft. high.

Sisteron marks the historical boundary between Dauphiné and Provence. During the Roman Occupation, "Segusturo" lay on the Via Domitian that linked the Rhône Delta to Italy. From the citadel built in the 11th Century and reinforced in the 16th with huge fortifications designed by an engineer named Errard, precursor of Vauban, there is a view of the vertical strata in the enormous Baume Rock which forms the southern end of the spectacular Durance Valley.

Top, left: Near the Verdon Canyon lies **Moustiers-Sainte-Marie** whose tile-roofed houses have been built at the foot of a breach in the limestone cliff. It is famous for its earthenware pottery (or *faïence*) for which the production techniques are said to have been imported from Faenza in Italy c. 1679. A few years later, c. 1740, Moustiers began to use the Spanish technique for producing polychrome pottery fired at high temperatures. The most famous decorative features are hunting scenes picked out in a range of blues.

Top, right: The **Verdon Canyon** cuts a deep gash in the limestone plateaux of Upper Provence over a distance of more than 12 miles. It is open to debate why the small river was determined to force a passage through this hard rock rather than flow round it. The theory of antecedence would seem to provide the key to the mystery. The Verdon was already flowing along this course when the ground was slowly lifted as a result of the formation of the Alps. Because of this, the river had no choice but to gouge out the rock, using natural crevices to assist it in its task. The gorge reaches a depth of 2,275 ft. in some places. It can be visited on foot (an all-day walk) via the "Martel Path" or by car along the Sublime Clifftop Route (*Corniche Sublime*).

Bottom, right: The impressively large outline of **Mont Ventoux** overshadows the entire area of Provence around the Rhône Valley. The summit (alt. 6,204 ft.) is subject to the fury of the mistral wind and the temperature is, on average, 12° C lower than the temperature in the surrounding area. The village of Brantes is beautifully situated between the northern slopes of Mont Ventoux and the limestone crest of Les Baronnies.

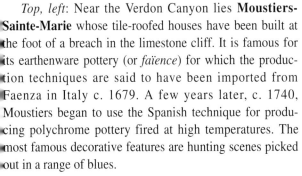

Top: **Gordes**, topped by a Renaissance castle and a massive church, has houses set out on a succession of terraces on the very edge of the Vaucluse Plateau opposite the Lubéron Range.

Bottom, left: The **Rustrel Colorado** not far from Apt consists of old yellow ochre quarries. Yellow ochre is a mixture of clayey sand and iron oxide. Vaucluse produces 3,000 tonnes of yellow ochre every year. It is used in the preparation of paints and distempers.

Bottom, right: **Vaison-la-Romaine**. The fomer capital of the Celtic Vocontii tribe was captured by the Romans at the end of the 2nd Century B.C. It quickly became one of the most prosperous towns in the Narbonnaise province and its population included a number of major landowners before it was laid to waste by the barbarian invasions. Archaeological digs have uncovered vast residences, a basilica, an atrium, and a theatre that catered for 6,000 spectators.

Right: The **priory in Ganagobie** was built in the 12th Century by the monks of Cluny on a plateau overlooking the Durance Valley, on the site of a monastery founded c. 950 by the Bishop of Sisteron. The church has a wonderful **portal** with ribbed archivolts alternating with festoons. The typanum bears a figure of Christ in Majesty, with angels and the symbols of the four Evangelists carved in a very lively manner. Underneath are the twelve Apostles. Inside, archaeological digs have uncovered a superb mosaic pavement.

Bottom: **Aix-en-Provence**. The former Roman colony laid waste by the Lombards in 574 A.D. regained its former glory in the 12th Century when the Counts of Provence established their official residence there. In the 15th Century, Good King René brought large numbers of artists to Aix and administered his lands efficiently prior to their annexation to France in 1486.

St. Saviour's cloisters adjacent to the cathedral (*left*) are a delightful piece of Romanesque architecture. On one of the corner pillars is a statue of St. Peter on which the

clothing and features indicate a very sure hand on the part of the sculptor.

The old town in Aix is a charming, elegant district with 17th and 18th-century mansions around the **Place d'Albertas** (*right*), cobbled courtyards, and a plethora of fountains.

Top and bottom: **Sénanque Abbey** (*top*) nestles in the midst of an isolated valley covered in lavender bushes. Founded in 1148 by monks from the Vivarais area (*p. 85*), it was part of the major Cistercian monastic movement, like **Le Thoronet Abbey** (*bottom*). The austere life demanded by St Bernard is evident in the architecture of the buildings with their plain lines and total lack of decoration.

Opposite, top: The castle in **Les Baux-de-Provence** crowns an isolated spur of rock to the south of the Alpilles. The Lords of Les Baux, whose authority stretched over almost 80 localites in southern France as far back as the 11th Century, were feared because of their immense pride and warring temperament. They were constantly in conflict with neighbouring powers and they rallied to the Protestant cause but Louis XIII got the better of them and ordered the demolition of the castle in 1632. The village (*p. 127*) has given its name to bauxite, an ore quarried in the vicinity from 1822 onwards.

Opposite, bottom: Jutting up from the middle of a vast stretch of marshland and lakes, **Aigues-Mortes** was built on the orders of St. Louis who wanted a fortress on the Mediterranean coast and a base from which to set off on the Crusades. In 1241, he had the original bastion built and it was there that he embarked in 1248 for the Sixth Crusade, at the head of an armada of 1,500 ships. The town walls were built in 1272 by Philip the Bold, two years after St. Louis' death.

theme of "Salvation". The creator of the bas-relief showing Abel making a burnt offering of a lamb and Cain presenting the Lord with an ear of corn gave his figures a linear movement which is a troubling reminder of the carvings on the cathedral in Angoulême (*p. 98*). Was it the same man?

Bottom: The **Pont du Gard** was used to carry 20,000 cubic metres of water across the Gardon Valley to Nîmes after it had brought this far via an aquaduct 30 miles long from a spring near Uzès. Built in 19 B.C. by the Romans, it has three levels of arches consisting of quarry-stones so large that they were assembled without the use of mortar. The arches have bonding made of separate stones, giving the bridge a degree of elasticity. In order to lift the blocks of stone, some of which weighed as much as six tonnes, a giant treadmill was used as a pulley. The water pipe was covered with a vaulted roof that served as a roadway and was designed to preserve the quality of the water, for the Romans were particularly careful in this respect.

Top: **Saint-Gilles-du-Gard** on the edge of the Camargue has a minster whose West Front marks a vital stage in the development of Romanesque carving in southern France. It was built in the mid 12th Century by several artists who were commissioned to illustrate the

Top: In the days of Antiquity, **Orange** was a Roman colony designed to cater for army veterans. Land was allocated to them and the town acquired a number of prestigious public buildings. The **Roman theatre** built during the reign of Caesar Augustus is the best preserved reminder of the days of Ancient Rome. The semicircle could cater for 10,000 spectators and the backdrop to the stage, a wall 335 ft. long and 117 ft. high, was faced with marble and mosaics. In the centre, dwarfing the stage, is a statue of Caesar Augustus.

Right: **Arles** on the banks of the Rhône and at the gateway to Camargue has a number of very interesting remains from the Roman Occupation and the town's revival in the 12th Century. The **Roman arena** (*centre*) is a vast oval measuring 442 ft. by 348 ft, built during the reign of Vespasian (c. 70 A.D.); it could cater for 20,000 spectators come to admire gladiatorial combat.

St. Trophime's Cloisters (*bottom*) are unusual in that they consist of two Romanesque galleries (east and north) built in the late 12th Century and two Gothic galleries added on in the 14th. The former have capitals "of a highly-developed form of Romanesque architecture, where every medium and resource is totally mastered" (*H. Focillon*).

Top and bottom: During the reign of Caesar Augustus, **Nîmes** acquired two magnificent buildings, both of which have survived to the present day in a perfect condition. The **Square House** (*Maison Carrée, top*) dedicated to the worship of the emperor was built to the same design as the Temple of Apollo in Rome. Its proportions, grooved

columns and Corinthian capitals are a reminder of Greek architecture. The **Roman arena** (*bottom*) is older than the one in Arles and, above the two lines of arches, it still has the attic bearing the pierced consoles that were designed to support the timber framework of a vast canvas sunshade.

Opposite: **Saint-Rémy-de-Provence** (*right*) owes its typically Provençal character to its bustling markets, ring of boulevards planted with plane trees and its fountains. The ruins in **Glanum** (*bottom*) stand in a splendid setting at the foot of the **Alpilles**. They show several different periods of construction. There is a Celtic town near a sacred spring which was extended by Phocaean merchants in the 6th Century B.C. Destroyed by the Teutons, the town was then rebuilt by Caesar and embellished during the reign of Caesar Augustus. Nearby are the **Antiquities** (*top*) consisting of a municipal arch marking the passage of the great transalpine route and a mausoleum erected in memory of Augustus' grandsons who had died at an early age. The base is decorated with bas-reliefs showing hunting scenes and battles.

Top and bottom: **Avignon** was a no more than small, prosperous town in the County of Provence when the arrival of the pontifical Court in the 14th Century, determined to shake off the pressure of the great families in Rome, changed its life and its appearance. The **Popes' Palace** (*top*) built by Benedict XII from 1334 onwards and completed by Clement VI c. 1350 looks like a feudal fortress. The interior, though, was elegantly decorated by the most brilliant Italian artists who came here from Sienna and Viterbe. **St. Bénézet's Bridge** (*bottom*) dates from the 12th Century but part of it was washed away in the 17th.

Opposite, top: **Marseilles**. Greek merchants from Asia Minor, the Phocaeans, founded a trading post in the Lakydon Creek in 600 B.C. This is now the site of the Old Harbour. Marseilles was born and with it, its maritime voaction which, over the centuries, made it the largest French port on the Mediterranean coast and currently the third-largest in Europe. The **Old Harbour** built in the shadow of the Basilica of Notre-Dame-de-la-Garde on which all the roads in the town converge constitutes the heart of Marseilles. It was brought wider fame thanks to the sing-song voices of Marcel Pagnol's characters, Marius and César, and the vividly-coloured, bustling fish market.

Opposite, bottom: Between Marseilles and Cassis, the **coves** and **creeks** dig deep into the limestone Puget Range. They are old valleys which were flooded by the sea when the ice melted in the Quaternary Era. The **En-Vau Cove**, which is accessible from the sea, has a charming little shingle beach lapped by limpid blue waters.

Top: At the end of last century, **Saint-Tropez** was no more than a modest port when famous artists such as Signac, Bonnard and Matisse set up their easels on the shores of the Gulf, attracted by the beauty of the natural environment. From the 1950's onwards, writers and film stars launched the resort and it has now become world-famous.

Bottom: The **Lérins Islands** (*bottom*) situated off Cannes and Golfe-Juan are covered with superb thickets of parasol pines and eucalyptus trees and edged with

minute creeks and coves. In the 4th Century, St. Honorat founded a monastery on the smallest of the islands; it was quickly to become one of the largest communities in the Christian world.

Opposite, top: **Nice**. The "pearl" of the Riviera is admirably situated on the shores of the Baie des Anges ("Angels Bay"). The vast shingle beach is backed by the Promenade des Anglais, the location of the most luxurious hotels such as the Négresco which was built in the Edwardian era. Entertainments and shows are organised throughout the year. There is the Mardi-Gras Carnival, the Grand Jazz Parade and the International Folk Festival in July, horse racing and water sports, and many, many more.

Opposite, bottom: The **Vésubie Valley** in the hinterland behind Nice has the advantage of enjoying the Mediterranean climate while benefitting from higher altitudes. In the middle of alpine mountains are terraced fields full of vines and olive trees, meadows and pine forests. The houses in the tiny village of **La Bollène-Vésubie** have all been built on the sun-drenched hillside overlooking the first mountain peaks.

Top: The **Principality of Monaco** is a sovereign State with an area of scarcely more than one square mile. Its privileged location in the heart of the Riviera and the absence of any direct taxation have attracted countless companies and private individuals, so that land has had to be reclaimed from the sea and buildings have had to spread upwards rather than outwards. Business tourism and the organisation of conferences are two of the main activities in the principality.

Opposite, top: **Entrevaux** lies in the Upper Var Valley marking the limit between Upper Provence and the alpine area. This corridor, which was of major strategic importance, was fortified in 1690 shortly after the outbreak of hostilities between France and Savoy. Vauban encircled the town with ramparts, linking them to the citadel by a single, enormous wall.

Opposite, bottom: **Menton** stands in a magnificent spot at the foot of a vast ring of mountains filled with orange and lemon trees. Two yachting marinas, several fine sandy beaches, and an old town backing onto the mountain make it a particularly attractive resort. The line of hilltops marks the Italian border. All along the Riviera from Menton to Nice (*p. 152*), the Alps plunge straight down into the Mediterranean. From the three hilltop roads, there are wonderful views of the most prestigious beauty spots along this stretch of the coast i.e. Cap-Martin, Monaco (*p. 155*), Eze, Cap-Ferrat etc.

Top: The **Porto Gulf** with its pink granite cliffs plunging vertically down into the deep blue sea is the most spectacular natural beauty spot in the whole of **Corsica**. The southern part of this cove, which is six miles deep, is formed by the "*Calanche*", an amazing landscape of rocks created by erosion.

Left: The **Church of San Michele de Murato** is a fine example of Tuscan-style Romanesque architecture. From the 11th to the 13th Centuries, Corsica was governed by the Republic of Pisa. This period of prosperity brought the island a plethora of religious buildings designed by Tuscan architects. San Michele, which was built at the end of this period (1280), is particular for its multi-coloured bonding consisting of alternating white limestone quarry-stone and dark green serpentine.

Bottom: During the period of Genoese domination from the end of the 14th Century to the War of Independence (1729-1769), **Bastia** was the administrative and economic capital of Corsica. The town grew up on each side of the old harbour. The tall houses and Classical West Front of the Church of St. John the Baptist form a delightful picture against the backdrop of mountains.

The archaeological site of **Filitosa** includes prehistoric remains that provide a huge amount of information about this period. The **statue-menhirs** were carved c. 1,500 B.C. by the **Toreans**, a maritime people who had turned to a more sedentary lifestyle and who had gained power and influence thanks to their technical advance (bronze, iron) over the megalithic peoples.

Bonifacio, once a Greek, then a Roman, trading post has houses set out along a rocky headland overlooking the sea, at the southern tip of Corsica opposite Sardinia. The white limestone cliffs 195 ft. high are battered by waves that are often storm-tossed.

TABLE OF CONTENTS

Hervé Champollion has travelled extensively in all the regions
in France over a period of fifteen years in order to take the
photographs that have illustrated more than one hundred books and
guidebooks. For this book, he set out on another 15,500-mile trip
through France, taking photographs, and gaining a closer insight
into the places with the greatest importance in terms of
geographical features, architectural style and tourism.
Hervé Champollion is represented
by the Top-Rapho Agency (Paris).

Cet ouvrage a été imprimé par Imprimerie Pollina S.A. à Luçon (85) - n° 66671 - B
I.S.B.N. 2.7373.1490.9 – Dépôt légal : avril 1994
N° d'éditeur : 2879.02.06.01.95